José Luis González-Balado is also the compiler of

In My Own Words
by Mother Teresa

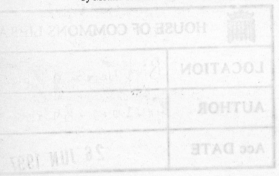

Mother Teresa

Her Life, Her Work,
Her Message

By José Luis González-Balado

Hodder & Stoughton
LONDON SYDNEY AUCKLAND

First published in Great Britain 1997, by arrangement with
Liguori Publications, Liguori, Missouri, USA

British Library Cataloguing in Publication Data
A record for this book is available from the British Library

ISBN 0 340 69422 X

Printed and bound in Great Britain by
Cox & Wyman Ltd, Reading, Berkshire

Hodder and Stoughton Ltd
A Divison of Hodder Headline PLC
338 Euston Road
London NW1 3BH

Millions call her Mother.
The best loved woman of the century.
A woman who lives for others.

CONTENTS

PROLOGUE

As a biographer and sincere admirer of her mission, I have always been interested in Mother Teresa. In this work I attempt to avoid what has been previously published. My intention is to present the life of Mother Teresa as a model of fidelity to the gospel through her love for the most needy human beings.

Gabriel García Márquez, recipient of the 1982 Nobel Prize for Literature, said more than once that he wrote so that his friends would love him. I do that as well, but more than that. I write so readers may love the person I write about: Mother Teresa. I also write for those who feel close to the work of Mother Teresa; I offer them further reasons for even greater connectedness.

Perhaps I do not appear sufficiently detached from the things I describe here to serve as a biographer of Mother Teresa. Greater detachment, however, is not possible, for I have witnessed or participated in some of the events I narrate.

With all I write in this biography of Mother Teresa of Calcutta, I am in intimate solidarity.

Part I

A PROPHET
FOR PEACE

Chapter 1

OUT OF INDIA

B efore her name was familiar in households around the world, Mother Teresa was quietly living out her passionate love for Jesus Christ. Long before the world came to recognize Mother Teresa's prophetic power, the abandoned, the neglected, the destitute, and the dying knew her gentle voice and warm embrace.

Fortunately for all of us, such profound goodness gradually gained international recognition and respect. The life of Mother Teresa of Calcutta may be, in fact, one of the greatest love stories ever told.

⏤

In the life and work of Mother Teresa of Calcutta, many persons, places, and circumstances can be described as "providential" because of the positive influence they had on the objectives to which she was committed. The list below is hardly exhaustive.

Naturally we note Mother Teresa's parents, Nikolle Bojaxhiu

and Drana Bernai, and her parish priest in Skopje, Albania, Father Franjo Jambrekovich, S.J. We also note those people who supported her in her formation and offered friendship to her while she was a Sister of Our Lady of Loreto.

In 1948, when this young woman consecrated her life "to the exclusive, free, and wholehearted service of the poorest of the poor," the following individuals were especially influential:

- Celeste Van Exem and Julien Henry: Belgian Jesuit missionaries in Calcutta
- Jacqueline de Decker: a Belgian citizen whom Mother Teresa called her spiritual godmother and also "my second self."
- Malcolm Muggeridge: a British journalist and Mother Teresa's first biographer
- James Robert Knox: an Australian ecclesiastic, apostolic delegate in India, later archbishop of Melbourne, and eventually, cardinal of the Roman Curia; a personal friend to Mother Teresa and an admirer of her work
- Eileen Egan, United States citizen and coordinator of Catholic relief programs to needy countries; one of the first persons to recognize and publicize Mother Teresa's work

Certainly we cannot fail to mention the seaport city of Calcutta in West Bengal, India, that so captured the heart of Mother Teresa. Without Calcutta, this woman's profile as "mother" would be incomplete. Although Mother Teresa loved the whole world and was happy to be in any city where, like Jesus, she "went about doing good" (Acts of the Apostles 10:38), she loved and identified with Calcutta.

England, Italy, and the United States (the country she most

often visited) each wielded a heavy influence on the mission of Mother Teresa. She never visited these countries as a tourist, however, but as an emissary for the poor, showing gratitude for the generosity of others toward them. Never begging money or material things, she simply shared her convincing human and religious example and sowed goodness by the handful. Her humble presence gave others the opportunity to prove the axiom by which she lived: "There is no greater happiness than to give yourself to others."

EILEEN EGAN

As a top executive at Catholic Relief Services (CRS), Eileen Egan had cause to frequent India, especially Calcutta. In that city of desperate poverty, CRS established The Works of Peace, a program committed to providing nutritional and health aid to mothers and children. Egan supervised this program.

During the course of her many visits to India, Egan met Mother Teresa and developed an admiration for the woman's courage and heroic Christian spirit. In 1955, Egan wrote an article that appeared in *Jubilee* magazine ("A Magazine for the Church and Her People" with a readership of one hundred thousand), describing the extraordinary work of this Albanian-Indian religious and her followers among the poor of the *busteess* (slum dwellers) of Calcutta.

The 1960 annual convention of the National Council of Catholic Women of the United States (NCCW)—a gathering of more than two thousand representatives from all fifty states—offered Egan the opportunity to bring Mother Teresa's wisdom and mission to the United States. Because the Las Vegas municipal authorities offered adequate facilities free of charge to the NCCW, the convention was hosted in that city of cabarets, casinos, and nightclubs.

In organizing and planning the event, special care was given to the selection of conference presenters. Feeling that it was worthwhile to bring Mother Teresa of Calcutta to Las Vegas, the NCCW left to Egan the task of convincing her to attend as guest and speaker. Providence supported Egan's efforts.

Egan was able to secure the support of Monsignor Ferdinand Perier, archbishop of Calcutta and the person whom Mother Teresa consulted for permission. He insisted that Mother Teresa accept the invitation. When Mother Teresa was presented with the proposal, she expressed her desire to visit the United States, not only to speak of her mission to the delegates attending the convention but also to convey her personal gratitude to a number of institutions and people who had helped the poor assisted by the Missionaries of Charity in India. She also wanted to take advantage of a stop in Rome on her return trip to facilitate the recognition of her congregation by the Vatican. Because such recognition was not official at the time, possibilities for growth were limited and the very future of the apostolate was uncertain.

THE JOURNEY

At that time, the professed religious of Mother Teresa's young congregation numbered 119. Some sisters had been with Mother Teresa for more than ten years.

Because it was small and in its infancy, the group of sisters required careful attention. In fact, the trip to the United States would be the first time that the congregation's foundress had left the community. She had remained close more out of maternal care for each of the sisters than out of a need to "guard" them.

Before leaving on her journey, Mother Teresa wrote a tender and encouraging letter to her small community. She told the sisters that at 5:45 A.M. on October 25, "God willing," she would board a Pan American Airways plane to fly to the United States and arrive there at 6:30 A.M. the following day. "I go, but my heart and my mind and the whole of me is with you. It is the will of God that I should go." She exhorted the sisters, "Let us be happy in spite of our feelings." She informed the community that Sister Agnes (her first follower) would act on her behalf in all matters, adding, "God will take care of you all, my children, if you remain one, if you love each other as God has loved you, with an intense love….I am not afraid to leave you, for I know the great gift God has given me in giving you to me."

In her letter, Mother Teresa explained that she planned to stop in Rome on her return journey to see the Holy Father. She would ask him "to take our little society under his special care and grant us a pontifical recognition," a gift, she admitted, they were not worthy of, but "if it is God's holy will, we will get it."

∽

Because this was Mother Teresa's first journey since 1929, when she had embarked for India from Albania, and because she had obtained Indian nationality, plans for the trip included applying for her first passport. Little did she realize that such a simple document would be put to much use, for this trip was only the first of many that the future held for her. No one could have imagined that future at the time, however.

This particular journey was fruitful in both short-term and long-term benefits. Eileen Egan says that despite the panic Mother Teresa exhibited at the prospect of giving a talk to such a large and select group in a land far from her home, this unknown nun from India turned out to be an unequaled public-relations spokesperson for the cause of "her" poor. It wasn't Mother Teresa's humble sandals and unfamiliar white-and-blue sari that captured her audience's attention or any rhetorical devices that she employed. Rather, her success came from the intense sincerity and faith that permeated her words.

In her biography of Mother Teresa (*Such a Vision of the Street: Mother Teresa—The Spirit and the Work*, Doubleday and Co., Inc., New York, 1985, and Sidgwick and Jackson, London, 1985), Egan notes a few anecdotes that Mother Teresa shared on that memorable occasion. For example, Mother Teresa spoke of a woman in the terminal stages of tuberculosis. After this woman entrusted her young son to Mother Teresa's care, she regularly traveled a great distance to assure herself that the child was well. Egan cites another example that Mother Teresa shared, that of a "brave and loving" mother who, after confirming symptoms of leprosy in her body, ran with her two-year-old son to a center of the sisters to find out if her son was infected with the disease as well. When it was confirmed that the child was healthy, the mother felt such immense joy that she forgot her own infirmity.

In her address to the NCCW, Mother Teresa gave testimony to the Missionaries of Charity and their service of love to Jesus present in the distressing disguise of the poorest of the poor. She shared with her audience the observation made by a high-ranking Indian government official who was neither Catholic nor Christian. "Mother Teresa," he said, "there is only one dif-

ference between what you do and what I do: you do it for Someone; I do it for something." Mother Teresa explained how the
presence of Jesus was central to her reply to this person: "You
are absolutely right. That Someone for whom we do what we do
is Jesus under the distressing disguise of the poorest of the poor."

Mother Teresa also told her NCCW audience that thanks to
the generosity of people all over the world, she and her sisters
were able to provide assistance to more than 74,000 mothers
and children. Rather than asking for donations following her
heartrending address, however, Mother Teresa surprised her
listeners with the unexpected. She said, "I don't come to ask
for anything. I have never done that since we began this work.
When I meet with a group of people—it doesn't matter if they
are Hindus, Moslems, or Christians—as I am now meeting
here with you, I simply tell them: 'I have come to offer you the
opportunity to do something beautiful for God.' And the
people give evidence of wanting to do something beautiful for
God. And they step forward."

Mother Teresa's speech, with her vivid anecdotes and dis-
turbing stories of impoverished conditions, inspired NCCW
members to return to their respective locales as vocal support-
ers of what they had heard. They were encouraged by the enthusiasm, compassion, and faith Mother Teresa had awakened
in them.

∽

Many of the contacts Mother Teresa made during this visit to
the United States proved important for her future work—and
for the people fortunate enough to meet her.

Among the people Mother Teresa met were two well-known

American cardinals: James R. Cushing, archbishop of Boston,
and Patrick O'Boyle, archbishop of Washington, D.C. Egan
tried to arrange a meeting between Mother Teresa and Cardinal Francis Spellman, archbishop of New York, during their
visit to the offices of Catholic Relief Services and the World
Health Organization, headquartered in the United Nations
building. Spellman was out of town, however, but Egan was
able to arrange a meeting between her humble guest and the
best-known of Spellman's auxiliaries, Monsignor Fulton Sheen,
the celebrated "archbishop of television," also known as "God's
microphone."

Significant as these meetings were, they were no more important than other unplanned encounters. For example, early
one morning, as Mother Teresa and Egan were leaving the
chapel at Leo House (a hospice for Catholic immigrants and a
"stopping off" place for members of religious orders in tran-
sit) where they had just attended Mass, the pair met Mother
Anna Dengel, a woman Mother Teresa had met in India eleven
years earlier and whom she esteemed dearly. Mother Dengel,
of Austrian birth, is the foundress of the Congregation of the
Medical Mission Sisters.

Mother Teresa's first meeting with Mother Dengel was
shortly after she left the Congregation of the Sisters of Loreto
in Calcutta. To prepare herself to provide adequate healthcare
to the poor once she established her congregation, Mother
Teresa sought medical training at Patna, where Mother Dengel
and her sisters managed a hospital and nursing school. Under
the tutelage of Mother Dengel, Mother Teresa proved to be a
dedicated student who learned far more than healthcare. For
example, she confided to Mother Dengel that once she established her congregation, she and her sisters would adopt the

diet of the poorest of the poor. With patient wisdom, Mother Dengel dissuaded her energetic disciple: "You shouldn't do that, Sister. You would soon be responsible for having sent your daughters to the cemetery, making them incapable for the service which they wish to render. Eat well and give them good food. In order to accomplish your service of love to the poorest of the poor, you need to be strong."[1]

Mother Teresa heeded the advice, and Mother Dengel made careful note of that fact when the two women met that fortuitous morning eleven years later. Following the warm exchanges of surprise, friendship, and wonder—having met in so unlikely a place as New York City—the old friends breakfasted together. Mother Dengel watched her former pupil enjoy a hearty breakfast beyond the means of the poorest of the poor in Calcutta.

Gratefully crediting divine Providence for their meeting, the two foundresses shared the details of their lives since their parting over a decade earlier. Egan was especially moved by the warm generosity, respect, and delight the women enjoyed in each other's company.

While in New York City, Mother Teresa also met Dorothy Day, the founder of the Catholic Worker Movement. Day took Mother Teresa and Egan on a "tour" of Harlem, the poorest and most violent of the neighborhoods of New York. Little did the world realize then that the nun dressed in a white-and-blue sari and walking through the poorest neighborhoods of the "city of skyscrapers" in the company of the former Marxist rebel of the twenties would one day receive the Nobel Prize for Peace and become one of the most admired and beloved women of the twentieth century.

Years later, in its December 29, 1975, issue, *Time* magazine published an article titled "Messengers of Love and Hope: Living Saints." Mother Teresa was featured on the cover and profiled inside with other "living saints," including Helder Cámara, Roger Schutz, Jean Vanier, Selma Mayer, Cesar Chavez, and Dorothy Day. The world press lost a prophetic photo opportunity that morning in New York when this unknown missionary to the poor quietly strolled along its most poverty-stricken avenues.

∼

During this visit, her first to the United States, Mother Teresa planted countless seeds of faith and compassion—seeds that would bear much fruit in the years to come. For example, Patricia Kump of Minneapolis, Minnesota, mother of four adopted children, had read Eileen Egan's article in *Jubilee* magazine and attempted to contact Mother Teresa while she was visiting the United States. Although Kump and her husband knew very little about this missionary of mercy from India, they had embraced her as their model of courage, strength, and Christian support.

Kump eventually reached Mother Teresa by telephone and thanked her for being a powerful source of inspiration. Mother Teresa, in turn, urged Kump to continue working for others and thanked her for her prayers. That simple telephone exchange was the beginning of a spiritual union between the Kumps and Mother Teresa; the Kumps became Mother Teresa's earliest Co-Workers in the United States and encouraged many other generous and enthusiastic people to join them.

When Mother Teresa prepared to leave the United States, she was far from "going home." Her return trip included several stopovers, Rome among them. Egan went with Mother Teresa to serve as her guide in a world relatively strange to her.

❧

At Heathrow Airport in London, their first stopover, Mother Teresa and Egan were pleasantly surprised to see Ann Blaikie, a friend and Co-Worker who had recently returned from Calcutta.

Blaikie had met Mother Teresa six years earlier when she and a group of other Western women, who lived in Calcutta because of personal circumstances, operated a store solely for the purpose of generating revenue for the poor. At the time, Blaikie was pregnant with her second child and unable to devote much energy to work in the store. The discomforts of the pregnancy, the suffocating hot weather, and the fact that she could contribute little to the operations of the store had made Blaikie depressed and restless. Someone suggested that she might feel up to making a contact on behalf of the store: look up a certain Mother Teresa who worked with the poor.

Blaikie accepted the suggestion, anticipating that contacting Mother Teresa would be a difficult task, but one hot afternoon shortly afterward, Blaikie met Mother Teresa when she was delivering toys to the Home for Abandoned Children (Shishu Bhavan).

After offering humble preliminary courtesies, Mother Teresa asked Blaikie if she would like to visit the orphanage to see how things were handled and to meet the children. Blaikie accepted in the hope that she would "catch" some of Mother Teresa's enthusiasm. The women also visited the Home for the Dying (Nirmal Hriday) that afternoon. Here, in this refuge of last hope, Blaikie knew that she had "caught" the enthusiasm for which she was looking. She committed herself to providing material support for Mother Teresa's efforts and to encouraging her friends to do the same.

Mother Teresa gracefully and gratefully accepted Blaikie's enthusiastic commitment to provide material help. She carefully pointed out, however, that serving the needy and the sick should begin with loving and caring for those in one's own family. She added that the children in her care needed bread, milk, and vitamins before they needed toys—and that even before bread, milk, and vitamins, the children needed love, affection, and companionship. In accepting Blaikie's offer, Mother Teresa told her that all assistance was welcome and was distributed to Christian, Buddhist, and Moslem children alike.

As she would tell others during her lifetime, Mother Teresa told Blaikie that she wasn't looking for people who would give money or material aid. Rather, she was looking for those who would give the most precious gift of all—themselves. She didn't want people who limited themselves to giving their surplus or leftovers or castoffs. For her beloved poor, she wanted that which is most meaningful to any human being—time—time to offer the gifts of companionship to the lonely, comfort to the sorrowful, and acceptance to the rejected. She wanted people to love and to see in the needy, in the marginalized, in the drunks, in the drug addicts, and in the sick what Christ taught us to see: "I was hungry and you gave me food…just as you did it to one of the least of these who are members of my family, you did it to me" (Matthew 25:35,40).

Mother Teresa spoke to Blaikie with conviction and delicacy, imparting a "lesson in charity" that Blaikie would teach

and model to others for years to come. The two women became good friends, and, years later, Mother Teresa appointed
Blaikie international coordinator of the Co-Workers. (The International Association of Co-Workers of Mother Teresa, as
such, wouldn't be officially born until March 1969.) Blaikie
and her husband, John, were present when Mother Teresa met
with Pope Paul VI because they had helped Mother Teresa edit
the original statutes for the lay organization that the pope ap-
proved and blessed.[2]

By 1960, when the two women met at Heathrow Airport,
Blaikie was fully dedicated to organizing Mother Teresa's work
in the West. Although John Southworth deserved tremendous
credit for aiding Mother Teresa's work and organizing Co-
Workers in the United Kingdom, Blaikie knew that it was the
presence of Mother Teresa herself and the "contagious" nature of her work that would most influence people. She remembered how she and her friends had been touched by the
power of love when directly exposed to the woman's presence,
and to her words. As a result, Blaikie and her volunteers approached Lady Hamilton, who convinced the British Broadcasting Company (BBC) to interview Mother Teresa while she
was in the United Kingdom.

Not only was the BBC the first television network to interview Mother Teresa, but it went on to play a major role in
giving thorough and consistent network television coverage
to the woman's work through the years. The one person who
contributed the most to making Mother Teresa and her work
known around the world was journalist and biographer
Malcolm Muggeridge.

Germany, the next stop on her return to India, had come to know of Mother Teresa and the Missionaries of Charity as a result of an article that appeared in *Weltelend* magazine. Barbara Bonk was a medical student when she read the article. Deeply moved by what Mother Teresa was doing, she asked to be admitted to the congregation. She wanted the opportunity to apply her knowledge and gifts to the sick, especially to lepers. Bonk made her religious profession of vows and took the name Sister Andrea. While in Germany, Mother Teresa wanted to visit Sister Andrea's parents. She also wanted to offer a personal thank you to Caritas (the Catholic relief agency) and Misereor (the Catholic overseas aid agency) for collecting large donations for her poor.

Mother Teresa's visit was especially gratifying for Sister Andrea's father, a retired Polish official, who seemed inconsolable following his daughter's decision to join the Missionaries of Charity. The words with which Mother Teresa assured him that his daughter was very happy working for the poor in Calcutta seemed to soften the deep furrows in his brow.

Mother Teresa also stopped in Geneva, Switzerland, to thank that country's Caritas organization for its help and to encourage its efforts to meet the needs of the poor. Like the United States, the United Kingdom, and Germany, Switzerland had responded with great generosity, placing in Mother Teresa's reliable hands those resources necessary for the ongoing work of a religious who was as exceptional as she was humble.

⸏

Mother Teresa was especially excited about her stopover in Rome, where she would attempt to "negotiate" final approval of the congregation she had founded. Because the congregation was functioning with only "experimental" permission, its activities were subject to the approval of local bishops. The bishops' reports to Rome about the congregation's work would bear on whether it was granted official permission. Naturally only positive reports would persuade Rome to consider approving the new congregation throughout the Catholic Church.

The Congregation for Religious, a department in the Roman Curia, addresses issues related to religious congregations and the so-called secular institutes. A separate department, however, the Sacred Congregation for the Propagation of the Faith (renamed the Congregation for the Evangelization of Peoples following the Second Vatican Council), in cooperation with other departments, oversees the relationship of the Vatican with religious institutes that have arisen in mission territories. The Missionaries of Charity fell into the latter category.

Because approval of the Missionaries of Charity was handled by the Sacred Congregation for the Propagation of the Faith, Mother Teresa met with Cardinal Gregorio Agagianian, an "Italianized" Armenian, in his office in the Spanish Plaza. Agagianian's sense of vision and wisdom had merited him serious consideration as pope in the conclave of 1958, when Angelo Giuseppe Roncalli (John XXIII) was elected.

When the moment arrived for her to be received by the cardinal, Mother Teresa carried no illusions of leaving with a signature of approval in her cloth bag. She had not counted on the slightly disquieting response she received, however. "As you know, Mother," the cardinal explained, "an ecumenical council has been convoked. One of the issues expected to be looked into is the renewal of religious life. As long as the council remains to take place and that issue to be discussed, the Holy See will abstain from approving new religious institutes. For that reason, it will be necessary to wait one, two, perhaps three years before it can be seen what the waiting period will bring about. Tell your sisters they should pray—and you also ought to—so that the Holy Spirit will enlighten the Holy Father and the bishops."

Although Mother Teresa did not accomplish her heart's desire, she left behind a legacy of humility and good spirit. One thing above all caught the attention of the hierarchy of the Roman Curia: the spirit of poverty powerfully evident in the Constitution for the Missionaries of Charity. The mother foundress not only planned for her sisters to emulate this spirit but she, herself, fully lived it.

It is interesting to note that John XXIII was pope when Mother Teresa made this historic stopover in Rome, and that, possibly, he had never heard of the nun from India who was igniting fires of love wherever she went. When the John XXIII Prize for Peace, a prize instituted in the pope's honor, was first awarded in 1971, it went to Mother Teresa of Calcutta. Although only the first of many awards she would receive, this one remains historically significant because of its association with two names so emblematic of goodness in the twentieth century: Mother Teresa and Pope John XXIII.

Also interesting is that, after Pope John XXIII died (June 3, 1963), two of his successors, Paul VI and John Paul II, met with Mother Teresa on many occasions and often initiated the invitations themselves. (John Paul I, who was pope for scarcely thirty-three days, did not have the opportunity to meet with Mother Teresa.) Many of their requests for meetings were to entrust Mother Teresa with delicate humanitarian missions. Both popes knew that such missions had their greatest potential for success when placed in the hands of the impartial and unsuspecting Mother Teresa.

～

While Mother Teresa waited several days to be received by the prefect of the Sacred Congregation for the Propagation of the Faith, she made good use of her time.

Thirty years had passed since Mother Teresa left her home in Albania to follow the demanding call of Christ. Although she had corresponded with her family over the years, contact had been limited because of her many obligations and the severity of Albania's restrictions on mail services. Her family was allowed to receive only one letter per month.

Lazar, Mother Teresa's brother, had qualified for a scholarship at a military academy in Austria because he was the orphan of a civil servant. When he finished training, Lazar entered the Albanian army as stableman for King Zog I. Shortly thereafter, Mussolini invaded Albania, and Lazar took part in the campaign against Italy and Sicily. When the war ended, he managed to settle in Palermo, Sicily, with help from Catholic Relief Services, and find work as a pharmaceutical products salesman. He married Maria, a young Italian woman, and they had one daughter, whom they baptized with the name of his younger sister, Aga (Agata).

When Lazar learned that his missionary sister from India would be in Rome, he made arrangements to meet with her. Because he had been kept better informed about their mother and sister, Lazar was able to share a great deal of recent family news that was unknown to Mother Teresa. She knew that both her mother and her sister had remained in Albania, which by then had sealed off its borders.

〜

Before Eileen Egan and Mother Teresa left Rome, Egan obtained invitations to a Mass celebrated by Pope John XXIII. In her humble manner, Mother Teresa did not request an audience with the pope, but not because she lacked a tender devotion toward the pope, whom she considered the Vicar of Christ on earth. Rather, she did not consider herself worthy of even a few minutes of the pope's daily schedule. Thus, Mother Teresa counted it a truly blessed privilege to be present at that Mass.

Chapter 2

A "PENCIL" IN
THE HANDS OF GOD

Eileen Egan, the generous witness and organizer of Mother Teresa's first journey to the United States, would write: "In later years, it became clear how this first trip out of India for an obscure nun of Indian citizenship was a foreshadowing, in the profound designs of God, of much in her future life."[1] It would be four years before Mother Teresa made another trip.

Meanwhile, the Second Vatican Council adopted guidelines for religious congregations that coincided with the spirit of Mother Teresa's Missionaries of Charity. The positive feedback that the apostolic delegate to India, Monsignor James Robert Knox, had personally given Pope Paul VI carried much weight in the final decision. This feedback also influenced the pope—a sincere admirer and benefactor of Mother Teresa—to take a symbolic action that reflected his high esteem.[2]

On December 2, 1964, Paul VI made the second pilgrimage of his papacy, going to Bombay to take part in the XXXVIII

International Eucharistic Congress. During that visit he traveled in a white Lincoln convertible given to him by a group of
Catholics in the United States. On December 5, as the pope
made ready to board the plane for his return trip to Rome via
New Delhi, he made an announcement that went far beyond
the obvious meaning of his words. Before television cameras
and a large crowd assembled to bid him farewell, Paul VI stated
that he would leave the white convertible as a gift to Mother
Teresa—"for her universal mission of love." Those words meant
the virtual approval of Mother Teresa's congregation.

Although Mother Teresa had been present for some of the
religious services presided over by the Holy Father, she was
not in the farewell crowd that cheered his symbolic generosity; she was attending to the dying elderly in Delhi.When she
heard the news from the apostolic delegate, Monsignor Knox,
she felt moved. She asked for a sheet of paper and wrote a
sincere and simple expression of gratitude to the pope, who
by then was back in Rome. Convinced that Paul VI would appreciate the informality, Monsignor Knox offered to take her
note of thanks to him personally.[3]

Paul VI knew that Mother Teresa was not going to keep the
car for her personal use; he knew that her beloved poor would
benefit from the gift in some way. The fact is, Mother Teresa
never set foot in the car. Instead, she built a self-contained
village for the rehabilitation of lepers with the proceeds that
she received from raffling off the car.

"A DROP IN THE OCEAN"

By the time the congregation received official approval (February 1, 1965), the Missionaries of Charity had homes in such

major Indian cities as Rānchī, Delhi, Ambāla, Bhāgalpur, Amrāvati, Patna, Raigarh, Darjeeling, Jamshedpur, Goa, and Trivandrum. Even so, Mother Teresa was aware of the magnitude of her congregation's mission; she knew that in the immense country of India, her congregation's efforts were no more than "a drop in the ocean."

With so much to do in India, and because God had so favored the birth of her work there, Mother Teresa was not eager to open homes in other countries. She lived convinced that she was no more than an instrument—"a pencil," she called herself—in the hands of God. "The work is not mine; it is God's." She remained ready, however, for whatever God asked of her, always alert to those providential signs that would direct her way.

One of God's signs "appeared" during a session of the Second Vatican Council. Among the 2,700 Council Fathers who convened over a period of four sessions between 1962 and 1965 were Monsignor Knox and Monsignor Benítez, the bishop of Barquisimeto, Venezuela. When Benitez shared with Knox his concerns about serious pastoral problems in his diocese, Knox suggested that Benitez invite a group of sisters from India to open a center for the poor in his diocese. The sisters, Knox said, would assist people in the slums most trodden down with spiritual and human misery.

Remaining faithful to the congregation's vow to tend to the poorest of the poor, Mother Teresa traveled to Venezuela in the autumn of 1964 to determine for herself the extent of the need there.[4] She discovered that conditions of extreme poverty did, indeed, exist in the West and that founding a Missionaries of Charity home in Venezuela would not conflict with her mission. Although the congregation did not yet have offi-

cial status, Pope VI expressed his support for Mother Teresa
to extend her work to Latin America and open her first home
outside India.

After a brief stop in New York to encourage local NCCW
groups to renew their commitment to the poor and to provide material assistance to the new Venezuelan project,
Mother Teresa returned to India. In July 1965 Mother Teresa
journeyed back to Venezuela to assess the progress of the
project and, providentially, her friend Eileen Egan met her
there.

Although Egan played an integral role in helping to establish the four sisters who would manage this new home, she
was especially supportive on the return trip to India via Paris,
Frankfurt, and Rome, where Mother Teresa attended to business relating to the congregation. In Rome, she also met with
her brother, Lazar, again and inquired about their mother and
sister who were living in Tirana, the capital of Albania. "I ask
God for no other grace than to be able to embrace you before
I die," she had written to Mother Teresa.

Lazar's attempts to get his family out of Albania had netted
no encouraging results, but his sister remained hopeful. "There
are kind persons ready to help us," Mother Teresa encouraged
her brother. "I am confident we shall accomplish it." In fact,
there were several "kind persons," and one of them was Egan.

First, Egan secured a promise on the part of Catholic Relief
Services to give shelter to Mother Teresa's mother and sister in
Italy should the two manage to leave Albania. Next, Egan used
her high-ranking position at CRS and at the United Nations
to persuade influential people to take an interest in the case.
As a result, appeals were made to the Albanian government by
the secretary general of the United Nations, U Thant; the min-

ister of foreign affairs of France, Couve de Murville; and by the secretary of state of the United States, Dean Rusk.

In spite of these efforts, the government in Tirana returned only the whisper of a reply to the French minister, who delivered the news to Mother Teresa and Lazar: "The physical conditions of Misses Drana and Aga Bojaxhiu don't allow them to travel outside the country." With great human wisdom, Lazar noted that the true illness of his mother and sister was "not physical weakness. What is wasting away their lives is the loneliness and the desperation of not being able to leave Albania and reunite with us."

Mother Teresa made one more effort. Accompanied by Egan, she went to the Albanian embassy in Rome, where she was received by a low-ranking official. Overcoming his initial suspicion, the official promised to bring the women's request to the embassy attaché and invited them to return the next day to receive a response. Their efforts were totally fruitless, as they learned the next day: "The attaché is absent from Rome. I regret to tell you that he has left no word for you."

Mother Teresa was never to "embrace" her sister and mother as she had prayed. Several years later, Lazar received a letter from Aga bearing the sad news of their mother's death. He notified his sister by telegram: "Pray for Mama; died past July 12." Two years later, Lazar found out that Aga, too, had died. Again, he telegraphed the news to his sister in India.

Mother Teresa anguished over not being able to lessen the sufferings of the two people closest to her. Yet, even her immense pain served the good of her beloved poor; the woman of mercy and compassion renewed her commitment to do whatever she could to alleviate the suffering of human beings. "Always, with love, I have obtained in life everything for which

I have asked. Unfortunately, there still exist barriers which love is not able to break down."

⌇

Mother Teresa's sense of her work as "a drop in the ocean" would *cross* oceans with Pope Paul VI's request that she and her congregation establish a home in Rome. Mother Teresa humbly reminded the Holy Father that her mission was to serve the poorest of the poor; she doubted that there was work to be done in Rome. But Paul VI knew of the existence of slums in the Eternal City. While an employee of the Secretary of State of the Vatican, he had walked through them on his rounds of charity with the Federation of Italian Catholic College Students. He assured Mother Teresa that beyond comfortable and elegant Rome there were, indeed, areas of extreme poverty. "Moreover, Mother," he added "even if there weren't any poor to work among, the testimony to poverty of your Sisters would be enough to justify their presence in our diocese."

Thus, in 1968, Rome became the site of the second non-Indian home of the Missionaries of Charity. In 1969 a third home opened in Bourke, Australia. This home was located in the Diocese of Melbourne, whose archbishop was the Vatican's former apostolic delegate to India, John R. Knox. In 1970 a home was established in Southall, a neighborhood on the outskirts of London. "A drop in the ocean" was beginning to produce a wide ripple effect.

SOMETHING BEAUTIFUL FOR GOD

As a result of the good "publicity" generated by Ann Blaikie, John Southworth, and others, awareness of Mother Teresa and her work spread around the world. Making a significant contribution to Mother Teresa's growing reputation was Malcolm Muggeridge's live interview of Mother Teresa, broadcast from the London studios of the BBC. An agnostic of Anglican background and not particularly interested in his guest—whom he knew only in passing—Muggeridge agreed to do the interview only because he was asked. Nonetheless, it proved to be a historic piece of work.

The interview was moving. Mother Teresa gave no hint of feeling special and limited herself to giving a sincere witness to her conviction that Christ identifies himself with the poorest of the poor. It was obvious to her audience and to her interviewer that her conviction fed her desire to see Christ, love Christ, and serve Christ in others.

The success of the interview led to the production of a documentary filmed on location in the Missionaries of Charity motherhouse in Calcutta on Lower Circular Road 58/A, in the Home for the Dying in Kalighat, and in the Home for Abandoned Children.

Despite her awareness of Muggeridge's professional capabilities, Mother Teresa was anxious about appearing before the cameras. The British reporter, foreseeing his guest's reticence, took precautions. He asked the archbishop of Westminster, Cardinal Carmel Heenan, for a reference. Muggeridge was convinced that few rationalizations would calm Mother Teresa's resistance like the comments of a bishop. To the outline of the script that Muggeridge gave him, the archbishop added that he believed the documentary "surely will do great good for souls."

The archbishop's supportive comments had the desired effect on Mother's Teresa's spirit. She relaxed and prepared for the filming. In her calmer state, she said, "Let's do something beautiful for God." This prophetic phrase became the title of not only the documentary but also a book, later written by Muggeridge, based on the documentary, *Something Beautiful for God* (Ballantine Books, New York, 1971). Both were key events in the spreading of Mother Teresa's image throughout the world, especially in English-speaking countries.

∽

Among those impressed with Mother Teresa and her work was Cardinal Terence J. Cooke of New York. He and Mother Teresa had an opportunity to visit in the fall of 1970, when she stopped in New York on her way back to India from Minneapolis, where she had once again addressed the National Council of Catholic Women. At that time, Cooke asked her to consider opening a home in New York.

Mother Teresa took the request into consideration, partly in gratitude for the generosity of the American people toward the poor. As always, respecting the congregation's constitution, Mother Teresa wanted to "visit the place to ascertain conditions of living and work." Although Cardinal Cooke suggested Newburgh, on the banks of the Hudson River, instinct led Mother Teresa, in the company of Egan and an official of the archbishop's chancery, to discover an area where social and human degradation were more evident: Harlem, an area in

South Bronx. Here she saw a desperate need that aligned fully with her mission.

The first home of the Missionaries of Charity in the United States was scheduled to be established in the spring of 1971, "God willing," as Mother Teresa always added to her promises—promises she then placed in the hands of Another. But the schedule was sidelined by a national crisis for India: the urgent needs of ten million people who burst through the Pakistani-Indian borders to seek refuge in Bengal following the ethnic-religious conflict that confronted the two western and eastern provinces of Pakistan in the first months of 1971. (This conflict precipitated the foundation of the nation of Bangladesh.)

Mother Teresa's delayed visit to the United States caused a number of last-minute changes. "Whenever a date was set for Mother Teresa's arrival in the United States," Egan wrote in *Such a Vision of the Street*, "a spate of invitations was generated. They were sent to me as the link with Mother Teresa." When Mother Teresa was unable to keep a scheduled appearance, the organizers of the event would usually invite the person who knew Mother Teresa better than anyone. This person would not be asked to *say* what Mother Teresa supposedly would have said but, rather, be invited to talk *about* Mother Teresa: her spirit, her witness. When Mother Teresa could not be present in Boston to receive the Good Samaritan Award from the National Catholic Development Conference in September 1971, for example, the conference elected to entrust the award to Egan, her virtual "delegate" in the United States. Such was not uncommon.

Among other programs planned to coincide with her visit to the United States in September 1971 were Mother Teresa's

acceptance of an honorary doctorate in Humane Letters from
Catholic University of America in Washington, D.C., and the
acceptance of an award from the Joseph Kennedy, Jr., Foundation.[5] Both events were postponed until mid-October, when
Mother Teresa could be present. Meanwhile, in September
1971, five Missionaries of Charity arrived in the United States
to operate the new home in the heart of the Bronx.

Strategically planned for Mother Teresa's rescheduled visit
to the United States, and contributing further to her prophetic
image, was the publication of Muggeridge's *Something Beautiful for God*. This move, which might have been of question-
able taste in other circumstances, was actually opportune.
Muggeridge not only showed no interest in making money
for himself (donating all royalties to the congregation) but also
gave clear indication that he wanted to commit his life to working with Mother Teresa on behalf of the poor. Muggeridge demonstrated his commitment by endorsing over to Mother Teresa
a sizeable check he had received for a television appearance in
the United States.

Establishing the Missionaries of Charity in New York brought
moments of humor and insight. "When we opened our house
in New York," Mother Teresa recalled, "Cardinal Terence Cooke,
a man who loved our institute a lot, showed his concern by
passing on to us a monthly fixed sum for the support of the
sisters: $500 for each one. I found myself facing a true double
dilemma. On one hand I did not want to offend him, but neither did I know how to explain to him that we accomplish our
work through the pure love of God and that we are not able to

accept any salary whatsoever. At last the way of explaining it to him more or less adequately seemed to occur to me: 'Pardon, Eminence, but I don't believe that New York will cause God to go bankrupt.'"[6] Mother Teresa added, "In fact, God has demonstrated it to us abundantly. We receive donations without stopping. I had come to the United States without a penny. By contrast, I have received…how do I know what I have received? I don't dare count all the money that I bring to our poor."

The sisters' home in South Bronx was established in a particularly violent area. From the very beginning, however, the sisters felt accepted and respected. "In New York, in the area where we live," Mother Teresa said, "conflict, suffering, and hate abound. Nevertheless, the Sisters go about wherever they wish without anyone doing them the least bit of harm. Our sari is for the people a sign of our consecration to God, that we belong to him. The rosary that we carry in our hand is a great protection, a defense, a help." Perhaps the most providential benefit of the home in the Bronx was the new mission that the sisters developed as a result of the social environment encountered there: visiting with families.

"Alerted by the neighbors," Mother Teresa said, recalling a particular incident, "[the sisters] arrived at the locked door of an apartment, from which there emanated an unbearable stench. When the door was broken down by the police, they came upon a woman who had been dead for four days. No one knew her name. Her case seemed like that of others: the residents of the same apartment building know nothing about their neighbors, except perhaps which floor they live on—and they know this only because their paths sometimes cross at the doorway or they happen to get on the elevator at the same

time. But they do not know them by name nor concern themselves with them except, perhaps, when the stench of their ca-
davers bothers them."

Mother Teresa drew this conclusion: "To those who say that
the Sisters do not accomplish anything spectacular in New
York, I explain that, although they may do no more than small
gestures such as these, it is still worth their labor. A person
who suffers, a poor person, is Jesus himself."

A WOMAN OF PEACE

By the summer of 1976, the image of the foundress of the Missionaries of Charity had transcended the narrow confines of
the religious and mostly Catholic world and had been recognized in the social and political spheres of the secular world.
That had been especially evident when *Time* magazine chose
her to be pictured on the cover of its end-of-the-year issue in
1975. Her message of love and mercy was penetrating humanity; it was heard as a call to peace and soon would be formally
recognized as such by the entire world.

Mother Teresa spent a great deal of time in the United States
in 1976. She celebrated Holy Week and Easter with her sisters
in South Bronx, took part in the annual convention of the National Catholic Educational Association in Chicago, and received an honorary doctorate from Loyola University. She also
addressed gatherings in Davenport (Iowa), Boston, New York,
Omaha (Nebraska), Tulsa (Oklahoma), and elsewhere. With
each appearance, Mother Teresa was presented with a humble
collected donation, although her audiences knew that they
could never really give enough.

In the summer of 1976 the episcopal conference of the

United States invited Mother Teresa to take part in its forty-first International Eucharistic Congress to be held August 1–8 in Philadelphia. Although Mother Teresa requested to be dispensed from any expectations to attend, Cardinal John Krol of Philadelphia felt that her presence would contribute to the success of the assembly. Before the congress began, Mother Teresa traveled to Mexico, where President Luis Echeverría Alvarez wanted her to open a home; to Guatemala, where Bishop Richard Hamm wanted her to open a home; to Madrid, in response to an invitation by Archbishop–Cardinal Vicente Enrique y Tarancón; and to Marseilles, in response to an invitation by the president of the French Episcopal Conference, Monsignor Roger Etchegaray.

While visiting one of the European cities, Mother Teresa held a press conference and revealed her plans to establish a new type of branch of the congregation in New York: the contemplative Missionaries of Charity. When asked why she planned this new branch to be established in New York, Mother Teresa responded, "Because in the United States they are prepared for the new Congregation; in other places, they are not." Cardinal Cooke was quick to approve.

Mother Teresa returned to the United States to attend the Eucharistic Congress and offered her address on August 6 to a most prestigious audience. It included Polish prelate Karol Wojtyla, the archbishop of Cracow (the future John Paul II); Father Pedro Arrupe, Prefect General of the Jesuits; Monsignor Helder Câmara, archbishop of Recife, Brazil; Father Bernard Häring, C.Ss.R., one of the most eminent Catholic theologians; Rosemary Goldie, an Australian member of the Vatican Commission for the Laity; and Dorothy Day. Her topic was "Woman and the Eucharist."

As was her custom, Mother Teresa did not review history or expound on abstract concepts. She simply invited everyone to recite the prayer of Saint Francis of Assisi, and then offered her humble and profound evangelical message—the message she repeated her entire life: "Jesus became like us in all things except sin. And he recommended to us: 'Love one another as I have loved you.'"

〜

Because media coverage of these events kept Mother Teresa's image and message in front of people around the world, her candidacy for the Nobel Prize for Peace gained steady backing. Campaigns to have her nominated for the prize began in 1972 and intensified in 1975: the International Year of the Woman. In the midst of these efforts, however, a voice of prudence arose to suggest that massive campaigns might not be the best way to assure Mother Teresa's nomination, that such tactics might actually be counterproductive; the Institute of the Nobel Prize Committee would surely resist such pressure.

In 1979 the Institute finally took Mother Teresa's candidacy seriously. With her cause championed by well-known public figures, such as Malcolm Muggeridge, Robert McNamara, Edward Kennedy, Lester Pearson, Hubert Humphrey, and Barbara Ward, she was chosen over fifty-six other candidates. Mother Teresa's long-time companion and supporter, Eileen Egan, was presumably responsible for much of the organizing that brought such respectable recognition to this humble yet powerful figure of peace.

On October 16, 1979, millions throughout the world received the news—news that had tremendous potential for fostering peace. The following comments from a devoted and generous Co-Worker from Rochester, Montana, captures the sentiment that gripped the hearts of a world desperate for mercy: "Of course, Mother Teresa does not need the honor for herself, but perhaps it will make many more people aware of her way of life: that of seeing Jesus in all his distressing disguises and serving him with a loving and willing heart in those around us."

Part II

THE SEEDS
OF GENEROSITY,
A HARVEST
OF COMPASSION

Chapter 3

CALLED TO SERVE
THE KING OF THE UNIVERSE

Nikolle Bojaxhiu, of Croatian origin, and Drana Bernai, of Venetian origin, were married in 1900. Although five children were born to the couple, the two oldest died shortly after birth. Lazar, the couple's oldest surviving child, was born in 1907; their second child, Gonxha (Agnes)[1], was born August 26, 1910; their youngest, Aga, was born in 1913.[2] Lazar was destined to leave the small Albanian family unit for a foreign country that he would eventually call home. Aga would remain close to her mother, and survive her by only a year.[3] (Both mother and daughter died in Tirana, the capital of Albania, where Aga was an assistant announcer on state radio.) Gonxha would eventually lose her civil identity to become universally known as Mother Teresa of Calcutta.

A CHILDHOOD OF TRAGEDY AND FAITH

Speaking to a group of married couples, Mother Teresa used her parents as an example of mutual love and fidelity: "My mother, whom I cannot forget, was a holy woman. She was busy all day. Nevertheless, when sunset approached, she hurried herself in order to be prepared to welcome home her husband, our father. At that time, we were not able to understand it. It almost seemed a joke to us, and we would laugh about it. Now I recognize what a great tenderness she professed for him and how delicate it was. It didn't matter what she had in her hands, she was always ready to welcome him with all her affection." She goes on to describe her family as "very happy and very united. We lived one for another."

Nikolle Bojaxhiu provided a comfortable living for his family. He was an enterprising man and a serious professional held in high esteem. His success had roots in family tradition; his father had been a good businessman as well. After working alongside his father and gaining a firm understanding of the business world, Nikolle, with an Italian associate, opened a successful construction supply store. Because his business demanded a great deal of travel, Nikolle was often absent from home but always returned to the open, waiting, and loving arms of his family—usually bearing gifts for his wife and children and sharing the tales of his travels.

While the children were still young, tragedy shattered this unit of love, a tragedy that is best understood within the political context of the time. In 1912 Albania gained its independence after five centuries of occupation by the Turks. Between 1914 and 1918, the country, although theoretically neutral, was a battlefield of warring powers that left nearly 70,000 dead.

Because Nikolle Bojaxhiu played an active role in his country's recovery efforts, he had a high profile as a nationalist and a councilman of the city government of Skopje. One November evening in 1919 at a meal following a meeting on national recovery, Nikolle was taken violently ill with gastric spasm. His condition worsened through the night, and he died during surgery at the hospital the following day. He left his thirty-year-old widow to raise their three young children: Lazar, twelve; Gonxha, nine; Aga, seven. There was sufficient evidence to suggest that Nikolle might have been poisoned.

Those who knew Nikolle Bojaxhiu well described him as a generous man who gave money and food to whomever needed it. "He never closed the doors of his home, even less that of his heart, to someone he knew needed food, shelter, or care," recalled an acquaintance. One elderly woman who frequented the Bojaxhius' door always felt particularly welcomed. "Treat her always with love," Nikolle told his children. "All the more reason in that she is a distant relative of ours. But even when they are not our relatives, we should always share our bread with those who have none. Never put in your mouth anything which you would not be ready to share with someone who is hungry."

Despite the comfortable standard of living Nikolle had been able to provide for his family, his death was as much a financial blow as it was an emotional loss. Upon Nikolle's death, his business associate secured for himself the family's share of the business, which left Drana to take on the role of breadwinner in addition to her role as mother. To provide for herself and her children, Drana worked as a dressmaker and weaver.[4]

"Our mother was a holy woman," Mother Teresa said of her mother. "She did all she could so that we would grow loving each other and Jesus. But above all else, she instilled in us the love of God. I remember when we were preparing for first Communion, she would teach us to avoid every lie, telling us that if we should tell one, our tongues would turn as black as coal. One day when I let one escape, I immediately ran to the mirror to look at my reflection. It could be my imagination, but I'm convinced I saw my tongue all black. Right away, I went to set things straight with her."

Mother Teresa's brother recalled, "Just as politics was our father's passion, religion was our mother's main interest. It was born from a deep conviction, which she wanted to instill in us. She demanded of us honesty, as much at home as in school. She wanted us to tell her everything we did and to ask for her permission before doing things. Without keeping us under her thumb, she was conscientious about her duties."

Lazar remembered how things changed with his father's death. "I don't know what would have become of us if it had not been for our mother. We owe everything to her. We ought to raise a monument to her....My mother worked miracles. She organized a weavers' workshop. She tried to make home life attractive to us, to keep us together. She was an extraordinary woman who almost did a better job than our father. She was less talkative but was no less effective. We lived right alongside the parish church of the Sacred Heart. Sometimes my mother and sisters gave the impression that they lived inside the church, going to the principal religious events and the missionary talks that so interested Gonxha above all."

During those difficult years, Drana shared her deep faith with her children. "Our mother had a temperament of steel," recalled Lazar. "She was a woman with a robust and firm personality. But she was, at the same time, humble, generous, sensible, and loving toward the poor, with a profound faith. She concerned herself a lot with our upbringing, which she accomplished more by example than by words. She was very orderly, and she liked good discipline. But what really stood out in her was her faith. Every night she gathered us together to pray. In May, she went with us every day to church to pray the rosary and to receive the eucharistic blessing." Above all, Drana instilled in her children the desire to share their possessions with the poor, thus sowing tiny seeds of generosity that would eventually net an abundant harvest of compassion.

⌒

Because Albania was predominantly Muslim and Orthodox Christian at the time, and because the school her children attended endorsed a nondenominational character in an attempt to foster religious pluralism, Drana gathered her family around the social and religious activities of her parish: the Church of the Sacred Heart of Jesus in Skopje, staffed by the Jesuits. Here, in this small community of faith, young Gonxha would socialize, participate in the parish choir, and encounter the first religious forces that were to shape her heart with a passion for the poor.

Father Franjo Jambrekovich, the parish pastor and a friend to the Bojaxhiu family, belonged to an order noted for its missionary zeal and commitment. Father Jambrekovich focused on the needs of the missions to nurture the faith of his small congregation. What's more, missionary work was in harmony with the mood of the church at the time.

Besides speaking about the missions, Father Jambrekovich circulated reading material that featured articles on the adventures of Jesuit missionaries in exotic countries, such as India, and that celebrated the "spiritual victories" of Yugoslavian missionaries in particular. Father Jambrekovich was noted for offering hospitality to any missionaries passing through the area, and he usually invited them to speak to the people of his parish.

Gonxha listened to these missionaries with delight. In fact, stories of the missions pleased Gonxha as much—perhaps more—than the stories her father shared about foreign lands. Through it all, this young woman's heart was being fashioned to hear the call to become a missionary herself. "I was still very young," recalled Mother Teresa. "I wasn't more than twelve years old when, in the bosom of my family, I felt a strong desire to belong to God."

It was, in fact, the glint of a religious vocation. Only her young age, and perhaps the counsel of the pastor, kept her from following the call at the time. She had to wait; she had to pray; she had to ask for light.

Although she did not miss the glimmer of a dream taking shape in her daughter's heart, Drana harbored concerns; she worried about Gonxha's health. Still, her own faith was to sustain her as she remained ready for whatever God might ask of her.

∽

Through the centuries, the Catholic Church has witnessed the birth and success of a wide variety of religious orders. History tells how each order has taken on its unique characteristics through any given era. Some orders, for example, have distinguished themselves by giving greater centrality to Mary, the

Mother of Jesus, and to the distinct "mysteries" of Mary's life. Others, the Franciscans and the Dominicans, for example, have focused on the model of a particular saint. Some orders are devoted to contemplation and mysticism, and others committed to active service. There are those that, without missing the order's main goal, have a greater capacity than others for adapting to the demands of the time in which they live.

Father Jambrekovich believed the climate of the church at the time to be ripe for the establishment of an institution for the young girls of his parish, one that would be "very special" to the Society of Jesus: the Daughters of Mary. The object of the institution was to foster a practice of those virtues most commonly associated with the Virgin Mary. Gonxha and her sister joined the Daughters of Mary, and both developed a deep devotion to Mary.

Also nurturing this faith in the Virgin was Drana's frequent trips, with her daughters, to the nearby shrine of Our Lady of Letnice. Here the climate was particularly good for Gonxha's health, and mother and daughters could stay as long as they liked in a small home that Nikolle Bojaxhiu had helped to build. Gonxha felt particularly happy during these times. She took short walks, read whatever fell into her hands, and asking for guidance, spent hours before the statue of the Virgin.

"It was at the feet of Our Lady of Letnice, near Skopje," Mother Teresa would recall, "where I seemed to hear for the first time the divine call. It convinced me to serve God and to surrender myself entirely to his service. It was the afternoon of the fifteenth of August. I was praying with a lit candle in my hands. That day, I decided to consecrate myself forever to God in the religious life. The scene, at the feet of the Virgin, remains indelibly [fixed] in my heart. It was the voice of God which called me to surrender myself completely to him by means of service to my neighbor."

THE CALL

In the late 1920s, a young woman contemplating the religious life as a vocation usually sought the wise and gentle counsel of her parish priest. Thus, Gonxha revealed her precious secret to Father Jambrekovich. Before doing so, however, she shared her heart with her mother who, in spite of her own deep faith, felt the piercing possibility that she might "lose" her eldest daughter. Years later, Mother Teresa said, "When I let my mother know of my desire to consecrate myself to God, initially she seemed opposed, but then she said, 'Well, my daughter, go ahead. Try to give yourself completely to Christ.'"

In *Such a Vision of the Street: Mother Teresa—The Spirit and the Work*, Eileen Egan writes: "When Gonxha confided to her mother the decision to become a missionary, the mother surmised that she was about to see her go away forever. Mother Teresa told me that her mother went off by herself to her room, closing the door behind her. She stayed there twenty-four hours. Certainly, she spent that time in prayer. Perhaps she shed many tears. If this happened, Mother Teresa never came to know about it. When she came out, her emotions were now under control. She found herself in a condition to be able to help and encourage her daughter to undertake the steps necessary to put into practice her decision. She gave her daughter a piece of advice that remained an indelible impression in her heart: 'Well, my daughter: go. Place your hand in the hand of God and never let go of him on your journey. Try to give yourself completely to Christ.'"

"I believe not only God but my mother also," Mother Teresa noted, "would condemn me if I did not follow faithfully my vocation. She will ask me some day, 'My daughter, have you lived only for God?'"

When Gonxha appeared before Father Jambrekovich, therefore, her mother was with her in full support. The exchange was challenging, promising, and, in its own way, historic.[5]

Drana: Father, here is the eldest of my daughters. She says that she wants to be a missionary and seems to be very serious about it.

Fr. Jambrekovich: It doesn't surprise me, Mrs. Bojaxhiu. I have always seen her as being more interested in these topics than any of her companions. Moreover, I feel free to say that she is one of the more serious young people that there are in the parish. But, do you know what this means, dear Gonxha? Are you sure that this is what God wants of you?

Gonxha: Father, before answering, I would like to ask a question. How can I know for sure if God is calling me, or what he is calling me for?

Fr. Jambrekovich: You will know it by your inner happiness. If you feel happy with the idea that God is calling you in order that you serve him and your neighbor, that's the best proof of your vocation. That deep joy of heart is like a kind of compass which indicates the direction which we ought to follow in life. We need to follow it, even when the compass might lead us by a path sown with difficulties.

Gonxha: If that's the way it is, Father, and surely that's the case because you understand the things of God better than anybody, I can tell you that for the past six years, since I was about twelve, I have been pondering over this subject. I have prayed a great deal to Our Lady of Letnice for light. I have arrived at the conviction that this is what God wishes of me. It's the only thought capable of making me happy. I think no other thing in this world would fill me so.

Fr. Jambrekovich: My daughter, it's not true that I understand the things of God better than others. But, yes, I think I understand your spiritual disquiet. Once I had it myself. That's why I am here, and why, before, I was in other fields of the apostolate. I also have been a missionary. Permit me to ask you, do you have a concrete idea of what kind of missionary you wish to be? Because not all are the same, as you well know.

Gonxha: Not much of an idea, Father. What I have read in the magazines you pass on to us refers more to Jesuit missionaries than to nuns. What they do to make the Gospel better known and to make Christ more loved stirs me inside. I know that women cannot do exactly the same things, but I suppose that religious sisters also can serve the poor for love of God and collaborate in the spread of the Gospel. Something like that is what attracts me. If possible, I would like to do it in India.

Fr. Jambrekovich: Do you realize that to do that you will need to go far away from Skopje and your family and that you will have to learn languages of which you have no idea?

Gonxha: I have thought about it, Father. I have thought many times that Mama and Aga, above all, will suffer much. That's what worries me most because I love them with all my soul. Now I have begun to ask Our Lady of Letnice to give me strength to overcome that worry and even more to give strength to them. But I believe that when God calls, one needs to listen, whatever the cost. If I am not mistaken, this is what you have preached on more than one occasion, Father.

Fr. Jambrekovich: Yes, I know, my daughter. It's easier to preach than to do. I also suffered much when I left home, and I don't know of anyone who has not suffered in order to follow his or her vocation. But your case is, under many aspects, more difficult than any. If you truly want to be a missionary and if you want to be one in India, I know a congregation that works hard and well, but they don't have houses of formation in Albania or in Yugoslavia. You would have to enroll in France or in Ireland. Can you imagine how far away that is?

Gonxha: Yes, I have with me a map of Europe. I know that Ireland and France are very far away. But if you believe that among those religious they may accept me, I'm ready to comply with the will of God.

Drana sat in silence through the dialogue between her daughter and the pastor. As she listened with anguish and tenderness, she didn't know which was greater, her sorrow or her excitement; Gonxha had said things that produced both feelings in her. After Gonxha's last response, she could no longer restrain herself. She had to share her concerns, and found her daughter's love and understanding especially touching.

Drana: But why go so far away, my daughter? Would it not be the same if you entered an order with houses closer by?

Gonxha: Mama, you know well...

Drana: Yes, daughter. I understand...

Father Jambrekovich then wanted to consider the practical details. He explained the procedures that Gonxha would have to follow.

Fr. Jambrekovich: You would not want to enter tomorrow, I imagine. First you will have to ask admittance and comply with some requirements. The first one, to tell those nuns your age. How old you are. I believe you must be around sixteen.

Drana: She turned seventeen this past August 26, Father.

Fr. Jambrekovich: A year older than I thought. That's better. The steps you need to follow will take a while because of the long distances the mail must travel. Moreover, I think that if we write them in Albanian, Serbian, or Croatian, we are going to make it hard for the sisters to understand us. I will ask a Jesuit friend of mine in Zagreb who knows English to translate my letter. If the sisters accept, we'll need to translate other documents for them: birth certificate, baptismal and confirmation certificates, good health certificate. You are in good health, aren't you, Gonxha?

Drana, speaking for her daughter, explained that Gonxha had bouts of illness, but she'd had only the flu in recent years. That seemed to satisfy Father Jambrekovich.

Fr. Jambrekovich: I will write and, as soon as they answer me, I'll let you know. Meanwhile, my dear young girl, don't fail to pray to God for light. Mrs. Bojaxhiu, I don't know whether to congratulate you or to tell you that I understand your sorrow. Perhaps the better thing would be for me to express both sentiments to you. You are a woman of faith. I believe you will be as convinced as I that one never loses a daughter whom one gives over to God.

Drana: Yes, Father, I believe that. But that does not help me to avoid the suffering.

Fr. Jambrekovich: Of course. For the time being, Gonxha will be good company for you while she waits. And Aga, who also is a very fine young lady, still is with you. Or am I mistaken?

Drana: No, Father, you are not mistaken, thanks to God. I am convinced that Kolle is praying for us from heaven. Perhaps he feels, up there, more happy than I about Gonxha's vocation. It's a thought that helps me to accept things.

Fr. Jambrekovich: Ah, by the way, how go things for your son, Lazar, in the military academy?

Gonxha: Apparently well, Father. That's what he tells us anyway in his letters. He has only a year to go before he is promoted to second lieutenant.

In her next letter to Lazar, Gonxha shared her news: she had decided to become a nun. Lazar, ecstatic at the thought of an upcoming promotion, took Gonxha's news as a joke. He replied mockingly, "Well. So you wanna be a nun—and among the 'infidels'! I guess our little sister is leaving us to be a missionary. Come on, get serious. Think about it a little better. There are better things for a pretty young lady like you, with a brother on the verge of being named stableman of the king of Albania. And, haven't you told me more than once that you would like to be a teacher?"

Gonxha did not care for her brother's glib attitude: "Brother," she responded, "you feel proud because you are about to enter into the service of a king with two million subjects. For my part, I infinitely prefer to serve the King of the universe."

⌒

Long distances and communication difficulties delayed a response to Father Jambrekovich's petition on behalf of young
Gonxha. But haste was not part of the family's agenda, not
even for Gonxha, who faithfully heeded Father Jambrekovich's
advice to continue praying for light and strength. She would
not change her mind. Although Drana saw the period of waiting as a good opportunity for her daughter to ponder a decision of such far-reaching consequences, she did not attempt
to influence the outcome.

Toward the end of the summer of 1928, Gonxha's plans came
to fruition, and the news was announced to the parish on September 23, 1928. Joyful expressions, tears, and hopes mingled
together as well-wishers gathered to celebrate with Gonxha
and her family. At a going-away gathering in the Bojaxhiu
home, Lorenz Bojaxhiu, Gonxha's cousin and the director of
the choir, gave Gonxha a fine fountain pen; "So that you do
not fail to write poetry," he said. "Also we expect a report of
your journey halfway across the world."

Everyone promised that there would be no crying during
the final farewell at the train station, but there were plenty of
tears. Even Gonxha, in spite of her efforts to control herself,
shed tears as the train pulled away from the station and her
family and friends disappeared from sight.

Drana and Aga traveled with Gonxha on the first leg of the
journey. After hundreds of miles through Kosovo, Serbia, and
Hercegovina, they arrived in Zagreb, where adequate lodging
had been prepared for them, thanks to arrangements made by
Father Jambrekovich. The three waited several days for the arrival of another Yugoslavian young lady, Betika Kanjc, also a
candidate for the missionary life in India.[6] Gonxha then bid
her mother and sister farewell and traveled to France and on

to Ireland with Betika. Drana, with her mixed feelings of joy and grief, could not have known then that she would never see her daughter again.

IN THE FOOTSTEPS OF MARY WARD

The scope of this book cannot examine each event in the life of Mother Teresa. Her spiritual relationship with Mary Ward, however, deserves special mention. Indeed, the life of Mother Teresa is not understandable without referring to the life of Mary Ward.

The foundress of the Sisters of Our Lady of Loreto, Mary Ward, was a seventeenth-century feminist pioneer. Pope Pius XII proclaimed her "an incomparable woman," and Pope John Paul II called her a "misunderstood woman...a perfect woman." He compared her to Saint Joan of Arc, Saint Monica (the mother of Saint Augustine of Hippo), Saint Rose of Lima, Saint Elizabeth Ann Seton, and Saint Brigid of Sweden.[7]

Ward prepared the holy rule of the Sisters of Our Lady of Loreto, which she modeled after the rule of the Jesuits. Her intention was to teach both the wealthy and the poor, which meant dispensing with the practice of "enclosure" (cloister) so the sisters could become "contemplatives in action." Her "innovation," however, was not well received, especially in Rome, where such a precedent was considered the exclusive privilege of monks.

Being in the vanguard cost Mary Ward a great deal. She was to see all her work undone and herself incarcerated by the Inquisition. Years after her death, her work re-emerged in Ireland from the hand of her disciple, Teresa Ball. In the archaic English of the time, the following inscription was carved on

Mary Ward's tombstone: "To love the poore, persevere in the same, live, dy and rise with them was all the ayme of Mary Ward who having lived 60 years and 8 days, dyed the 20 of Jan. 1645."

This was the spirituality that welcomed young Gonxha and Betika to Rathfarnham, near Dublin, in October 1928. After complying with legal procedures for entering a country that was part of the British Empire at the time, Betika and Gonxha dedicated themselves to learning English, the official language of the Sisters of Our Lady of Loreto—and of India—and to familiarizing themselves with the person and the work of Mary Ward. At the end of two months, the young women were sent to India for formation.

∽

The ship *Marcha* set sail on December 1, 1928, for a voyage that would last over a month. Young Gonxha and Betika spent the feast of Christmas on board, but on December 27, they docked in Colombo, the capital of Ceylon (today's Sri Lanka), where passengers were able to celebrate Mass. The ship finally entered the mouth of the Ganges River on January 6, 1929, the feast of the Epiphany, which the Church interprets as symbolic for the missions.

After so many journeys in such a short period through many different cultures, young Gonxha must have been awash with confusing emotions as she set foot on the soil of yet another foreign land. Far from her simple origins of Skopje, she was facing many unknowns. Surely she must have suffered homesickness. Although her brief stay with the Sisters of Our Lady of Loreto at Rathfarnham had been a gentle introduction to ethnic diversity, nothing could have prepared her for Calcutta.

A city unique unto itself, a city one never forgets—this is the essence captured in a description of Calcutta written by Mario Bertini, an Italian Co-Worker:

> "Much literature has been written and many movies have been made about [Calcutta], but as valid as those testimonies are, there still is a desire to add more.…The finest writers and the best reporters never will be able to bring alive the perfumes and the stenches, the sounds and the noises, nor the smells of Calcutta. When one sees this city one time, one carries it upon one's shoulders for the rest of his life, as much in the body as in the soul.… Calcutta, this inferno of a thousand contradictions where thousands of creatures, from the prematurely born to the dying aged, are seen rejected daily by the 'organized' man."

Although Gonxha was in Calcutta for only a week, the city made a strong initial impression on her.

∽

From Calcutta, Gonxha went to Darjeeling, situated on the slopes of the Himalayas. The city boasted an ideal climate and served as a summer retreat for the rich of Bengal. Here, Gonxha was first immersed into the environment that was destined to mark important moments in her life as a Sister of Loreto. Her two-year novitiate—a period of training and formation, soul-searching and prayer, study and discipline—brought her to the profession of vows on May 25, 1931. In vows of chastity, poverty, and obedience, she consecrated herself to God: she would not give over her heart to human affections or contract marriage; she would renounce personal property and the use of material goods beyond those necessary for living in austerity in community; she would submit herself to the authority of her superiors.

When a young novice makes her profession, she transfers her juridic loyalty to the institute, symbolized by the habit she receives. Gonxha received the standard habit for the Sisters of Loreto: black with a white veil and cap. Even more symbolic than the donning of a habit, however, was a change in name. Gonxha renounced the name she had been given twenty years earlier, and chose to call herself Teresa after Saint Thérèse of Lisieux (of the Child Jesus). Although Father Edward Le Joly, a reliable Jesuit source, observes that Mother Teresa often celebrated her feast on the fifteenth of October (the feast of Saint Teresa of Ávila), Mother Teresa herself, at the founding of the Missionaries of Charity, was most explicit about her name: "I chose to call myself Teresa. But it wasn't after the name of the great Teresa of Ávila. I chose the name of the little Teresa; Thérèse of Lisieux."

These first vows had an annual character to them. At the end of the first year, the candidate had an opportunity to reconsider her vocation and choose not to continue her profession further. Young Sister Teresa, however, suffered no wavering, not before her profession as a novice or during her period of temporary vows. What's more, her superiors had no doubt about the young woman's calling to the religious life and her suitability to teaching, the main mission of the Sisters of Loreto.

Thus, shortly after the profession of her final vows, young Sister Teresa was assigned to a teaching position in Calcutta.

～

In this city of misery and affluence, no geographic lines separate the economic classes; misery and wealth rub shoulders. At different points along the same street in the same neighborhood, one can find both luxurious and shamefully miserable homes.

The Sisters of Loreto operated two high schools in the city, both on the same great estate. One school met the needs of the poor; the other met the needs of the wealthy. Both schools were staffed by sisters of high professional qualifications who were subject to equally high religious norms and ideals. One school, called Loreto Entally, provided free schooling to girls from the slums of the city; the other, called Saint Mary's High School, charged tuition. Its students were Bengali and colonial middle-class girls.

Sister Teresa, obedient to the authority of her superiors, taught at Saint Mary's. Her primary focus was geography and history, although she taught other subjects as the need arose. Her warm enthusiasm and contagious joy won her the esteem of her peers and the affection of her students, so much so that she was promoted to the position of headmistress after a few years.

Sister Teresa's devotion to her teaching tasks left little time for anything else. She did not, however, fail to remain in contact with her family who, by that time, had moved to Tirana, the capital of Albania. "Dearest Mama," she wrote, "I am so sorry to be so far away from you, but I beg you to be happy, as is your daughter, Gonxha. Life here is very different from life over there. The high school I'm at is very pretty. I'm a teacher. I like teaching very much. I feel very loved here. Recently the high school named me dean of studies. But I'm the same as always."

Drana took a great deal of comfort in the fact that her daughter seemed happy and that their prayers for one another kept the family together in spirit. Although Drana missed Gonxha deeply, she supported the vocation to which her daughter had been called. She encouraged her daughter: "My dear daughter: Never forget that the only reason for your going forth to a country so far away was the poor." Sister Teresa did, indeed, remember the poor.

THE WINDS OF CHANGE

In the mid forties, events of great magnitude were taking place in India. For more than three hundred years, the Indian subcontinent had been harshly governed by Great Britain. In the period following the end of the Second World War, the long fight waged by India to free itself from British domination found a leader equipped to deal with India's multicultural composition: Mahatma Gandhi. Describing the conditions under which India gained independence within the British Commonwealth as "something worse than an error: a crime, a sin," Gandhi would eventually lose his life in the effort to heal the human wounds of political strife.

It was inevitable that the effects of political unrest—hunger, violence, and paralyzing fear—would penetrate the solid walls of Loreto Entally and Saint Mary's High School. The parents of many of the students, in fact, were active participants in the conflict. Trying not to alarm their students, the teachers invited open dialogue about the atmosphere of fear that gripped their country and the desires for peace that everyone shared.

It is safe to assume that Sister Teresa felt tremendous sympathy for Gandhi—to a much larger degree than the majority of women in her community who were of Irish origin. After all, her own homeland, Albania, had suffered foreign domination for centuries. What's more, she understood the plight of the victims of war, and that's the "side" she would always choose: the poor, the sick, the most defenseless. She taught her students that surrendering to the needy was a genuine expression of faith, and she modeled this faith by inviting her students to go with her to visit the poor in the parish surrounding the Loreto Entally property.

Encountering the savage fruits of war and witnessing first-hand the miserable poverty of the entire city of Calcutta, Sister Teresa began to feel the winds of her soul stirring her toward a change. As she heard these first whispers of a call to total self-surrender to the service of the poor, she exercised a certain amount of boldness. On one occasion, for example, there was a week of general strikes, widespread panic, and strictly enforced curfews. Although Sister Teresa was among the first to suggest that Loreto obey the restrictions, her passion to help eventually overcame any sense of risk. She asked her direct superior for permission to leave the compound to see to the needs of the poor. After an initial hesitation, and with due concern for Sister Teresa's welfare, the superior granted the request. No harm came to young Sister Teresa, and a few victims of poverty felt the generous goodness of God. Thus, a precedent was set that ushered in many more such rendezvous—and through it all, Sister Teresa's call to a mission of charity grew ever deeper.

⌐

During the two nerve-wracking years of the Gandhian struggle for independence, Sister Teresa experienced a vocational "crisis," not in the sense of doubt but in a deepening of faith. It's not that the young woman felt herself pulled off course; rather, she knew that she was somehow called to a more profound experience of her vocation. Her love and esteem for her sisters remained constant; by no means did she believe that the call she felt made her better in any way.[8] She simply knew that God was calling her toward something different.

Sister Teresa did not claim that her inspiration took place during a pseudomystical rapture in a sacred place. Rather, it took place on a crowded and slow-moving train traveling from Calcutta to Darjeeling in September 1946. She was going to Darjeeling, where each sister went once a year, to engage in eight days of spiritual exercises. Most likely, she was not traveling alone; the Constitution of the Sisters of Loreto prohibited such a thing. In spite of this, there is no evidence that her companion or companions noticed anything out of the ordinary.

Sister Teresa shared her experience with only a few persons: Father Celeste Van Exem, her Jesuit spiritual director; Father Julien Henry, a Jesuit missionary in Calcutta; and her superior. "Pray, ask for God's light. We shall pray for you and with you" was the advice she received.

Already praying for guidance, Sister Teresa intensified her prayer, remained faithful to her tasks as a Sister of Loreto, and made a concentrated effort to conceal her anxiety so as not to cause any distress to those she deeply cared about. She knew that if the topic was uncomfortable for her, it would certainly be the same for others. What's more, she wasn't sure of her response to the experience: "I knew where I had to go but not how to get there." She knew the end but not the means. She knew, too, that she would ultimately have to leave the Sisters of Loreto, where she had been content and happy for nearly twenty years. But her heart heard her mother's words so often repeated throughout her childhood: "Just as you did it to the least of those who are members of my family, you did it to me" (Matthew 25:40). She wanted to be faithful but knew that fidelity would not make anything easier for her. Yet, fidelity to her conscience and to God's will enabled her to venture ahead. Through it all, she grew to love her community even more.

A year later Sister Teresa still felt the inspiration in her inner being as she again made the spiritual exercises in September 1947. As during the previous year, she returned to her spiritual director, Father Van Exem, and contacted her provincial superior. The superior suggested that Sister Teresa contact the superior general but continue to keep the issue concealed from the other sisters and from her students.

In the meantime, Father Van Exem discussed the matter with the archbishop of Calcutta, Ferdinand Perier, also a Belgian Jesuit and a friend of Father Van Exem. The topic was painful and troublesome: one of the diocese's finest religious, and the principal of a Catholic girls' high school, might "leave" the order. The superior dreaded the possible loss and the fact that such events usually produced a certain alarm. Both the superior general and the archbishop, however, realized that no human conjectures could legitimatize putting obstacles in the path of God's will, of which there was moral evidence.

To follow her passionate call, Sister Teresa had to comply with the rigorous ecclesiastical legislation in effect at the time, which meant she had to secure permission from the pope to leave the Sisters of Loreto. Both Archbishop Perier and Superior General Mother Gertrude Kennedy endorsed Sister Teresa's plans, only vaguely aware of the sacred duty they exercised. In February 1948, Father Van Exem advised Sister Teresa about the letter she sent to Pope Pius XII through the Vatican delegation in Delhi.

The wait began. Through the long spring months and into the summer, Sister Teresa heard no reply. Finally, near the end of July, a reply arrived—postmarked the middle of April. The mysterious delay, however, did not detract from the impact of the response. The Vatican authorized an experimental exclaustration (permission to live outside the cloister) for Sister Teresa: she was granted permission to leave the Sisters of Loreto but was to remain a vowed religious woman under the direction of Archbishop Perier. When informing Sister Teresa of the pope's response, Mother Gertrude Kennedy assured Sister Teresa that, if she changed her mind, she should not hesitate to return to Loreto, where she would be welcomed with open arms.

Chapter 4

HEART AND HANDS
TO THE TASK

For Mother Teresa the celebration of the Assumption of the Virgin Mary on the evening of August 15, 1948, ordinarily a festive feast, was laced with sadness. Although she was at the point of finishing an agonizing wait, Sister Teresa felt little joy. She would later admit that leaving Loreto was far more painful than leaving her family nearly twenty years earlier.

Millions of people would come to know Mother Teresa of Calcutta in later periods of her life, when she seemed clothed in an aura of peace and triumph, with projects in full expansion. But on the afternoon of August 16, 1948, Sister Teresa left Loreto as an unknown, with no more than a small suitcase and five rupees. She was a young thirty-eight-year-old religious entering the future with the single weapon of her immense faith.

THE BIRTH OF A CONGREGATION

Sister Teresa's first hours in the city were desperate. Within a short period of time, she gave four of her five rupees to a poor man, and the last to a priest who approached her with a money box: "Sister, would you not also like to help out with a small offering in favor of good reading?" With nothing left but her small suitcase and a few personal belongings, she continued to walk in the direction of the train station at Hawrah.

Sister Teresa's faith did not falter, but her strength did. In her first night outside the secure environs of Loreto, she was tempted to go back. She overcame her feelings, however, by reflecting on how loneliness and the lack of basic necessities must weigh on the poor. She garnered strength from an inner sigh that confirmed her decision: "My God, I feel weak. I feel I lack everything. Come to my aid. You! Only you, Lord!"

To avoid the loving curiosity of her former students, Sister Teresa heeded the advice of her spiritual director to leave the city of Calcutta for a brief time. Realizing that she needed training in medicine to best serve the poor, she took a train to Patna and studied at the school for nurses of the Medical Mission Sisters annexed to the Hospital of the Holy Family.

There, where she felt well received, Sister Teresa shared her passion for serving the poorest of the poor. Anna Dengel, the mother superior of the Medical Mission Sisters and a specialist in surgery, became her confidante and listened with enthusiasm and interest. In this atmosphere of support, Sister Teresa grew in wisdom and prudence regarding many of the details that eventually would fashion the congregation she would birth. Years later, when Mother Teresa and Mother Dengel met in New York City, the two would remember fondly this time of formation, education, and spiritual growth.

~

In December 1948, after several months of medical training and a retreat under the direction of Father Van Exem, Sister Teresa returned to Calcutta to enter fully the world of the poor. Lodging with the Little Sisters of the Poor at Saint Joseph's Asylum for the Elderly, she set out each morning, with a sandwich in her pocket, to work in the slums among the abandoned. The sandwich usually became someone else's lunch, which left the tireless nun fasting until her return to the asylum. Her streetcar money often disappeared the same way: someone needed food or clothing or medicine. It wasn't unusual for Sister Teresa to walk home on an empty stomach. Her mission had begun.

One of her goals in those early days was to find her own lodging, something that offered no more than her beloved poor enjoyed. Supporting her efforts were Father Henry, the pastor of the parish of Saint Teresa, and Father Van Exem. One day, after taking Communion to Michael Gomes's mother, Father Henry casually asked Michael if he knew "anyone who might make available an empty lodging to rent to a very fine person, a Sister of Loreto, who has gotten permission to live outside the convent and to dedicate herself completely to serve the poor." Michael's daughter, a student at Loreto Entally and aware of the nun who had "abandoned teaching for who knows what," suggested that her father consider offering the third floor of their home, a space that had been unoccupied for some time. "It seems a little large," Father Henry commented upon inspection, "but unless there is something else the matter, it might do." They decided to let Sister Teresa decide for herself. Thus, hoping that someone would soon share this newfound space with her, Sister Teresa moved into her small apartment at Greek Lane 14. She didn't have long to wait.

One day, Subashini Das, a former student of Sister Teresa, knocked at her door.[1] "Mother, if you admit me, I would like to join you in serving the poor," she offered.

"If you are convinced that God is calling you," responded Mother Teresa, "I do not have the right to reject you. But first you must be thoroughly convinced of that. This will be difficult. I see, for instance, that you are wearing a very pretty sari. Your family is economically well off. Here, you would have to renounce everything, and yourself as well, to serve God in the poor. Think about it and pray. I will pray for you."

Some weeks later, on the feast of Saint Joseph, Das returned, determined to follow her former teacher regardless of the sacrifices. She was willing to adopt the same type of modest blue-and-white sari that Sister Teresa donned and to embrace the austere lifestyle that spoke of solidarity with the poor. Thus were the humble beginnings of the Missionaries of Charity. More women were to follow in Das's path.

During the first two years, the community of women grew to ten, then twenty-eight—many of them Sister Teresa's former students from Loreto. They remained in the section of the house that Michael Gomes had put at their disposal rent free. One of them, a niece of Michael Gomes, originated the name, "community of Missionaries of Charity in heaven."

Before the period of exclaustration was completed, Rome implicitly authorized its extension. In fact, on October 7, 1950, in answer to a request by Archbishop Perier, the Holy See gave the green light for the former Sister of Loreto to begin a religious congregation called Missionaries of Charity. Its purpose was to serve the poorest of the poor, and the sisters soon needed more room.

With the provisional diocesan character of the new congregation placed under his supervision, Archbishop Perier was eager to support the Missionaries of Charity. He prevailed upon Father Henry and Father Van Exem to search for larger, more private lodgings for Mother Teresa and her followers.

The priests found Lower Circular Road No. 54, a residence not far from Michael Gomes's house. It belonged to a Moslem who had been a Justice Department official, and he sold the residence at a reasonable price when he found out who the new tenants would be. The vicar general, Monsignor Eric Barber, in the name of the archdiocese, paid for the property.[2] That building became both the motherhouse and headquarters of the Missionaries of Charity.

NIRMAL HRIDAY

Only a few months prior to the acquisition of the motherhouse/ headquarters of the congregation, Mother Teresa embarked on a project that constitutes one of the most astonishing enterprises that she ever accomplished.

The passion for her project evolved as she attempted to assist the abandoned dying, those people who have no place to go to exhale their last breath. In Calcutta, there are thousands of such human beings; they are born in the street, live in the street, and eat—the little they manage to scrape together—in the street. In the street they contract illnesses, and in the street they die.

Mother Teresa found one of these people—half-eaten by rats, lying in the rain on the sidewalk, ignored by passersby, and dying. After carrying the woman to several nearby hospitals, where she was repeatedly refused admission, Mother Teresa watched the woman die in her arms. While she recommended the woman's soul to God, she was distraught by the merciless rejection to which the poor woman had been subjected. "What we would not have done to a domestic animal, we do to a human being!"

With that experience burning in her soul, Mother Teresa, still a complete unknown, immediately went to see the mayor of Calcutta to express her concern for the abandoned people dying in the streets. Because she had applied and received Indian citizenship shortly after leaving Loreto, she was able to speak on behalf of the citizens of "her" country. Respectfully holding back her own deep emotions, Mother Teresa simply described the situation of the dying homeless and asked for a place where she could take care of them. She assured the city's officials that she wanted only a location; she and her sisters would do the rest. Her conviction and insistence persuaded them to help her.

The city offered Mother Teresa a choice of two locations. She decided against the "nicer" location because it was situated in an area rarely visited by the poor. Instead, she chose the other site, Kalighat's *dormashalah*, a place of free lodging for pilgrims from outside Calcutta who came to visit the goddess Kali. The place was dirty, in extremely poor repair, and attracted a great deal of prostitution and crime. Had city officials been sufficiently interested to ask Mother Teresa about her choice, they would have found her reasoning consistent with her faith. She preferred the sacred character of the *dormashalah,* albeit a sacredness different from the Catholic Christian character, because she knew that most Indians would prefer to die under the gaze of the protector goddess of the city.

It was precisely the *dormashalah*'s sacred character, however, that created problems for the municipal authorities. Many considered it a profane exercise; others feared losing control of an area ideally suited for illegal trafficking. The authorities followed up on these objections by entrusting the chief of police to investigate the situation. He did so in an impartial manner, and his findings made light of the issues supposedly at stake. "Gentlemen," he concluded, "I am ready to block the work in these premises, but only under the condition that your mothers or sisters come to do what that sister is doing."

The priests of the goddess Kali were also annoyed with Mother Teresa, so much so that their ill feelings drove them to the point of conspiring to kill her. When one of the priests became ill to the point of death, however, he found himself abandoned except for the care and compassion offered by Mother Teresa. "Until now I have served the goddess Kali depicted in an idol," the dying man admitted. "I assure you, that nun is the goddess Kali in person." In the face of such gentle goodness, the priests of Kali eventually allied themselves with Mother Teresa.

∽

Mother Teresa named this place of last refuge Nirmal Hriday, which means "home of the pure heart." Inaugurated on August 22, 1954, Nirmal Hriday includes the goddess Kali temple grounds, the nearby buildings, and the spaces that constitute the sacred area. This harbor represents the zenith of unconditional self-giving where thousands, who otherwise would have died in the streets under the indifferent gaze of other human beings, have died in comfort and dignity.

Nirmal Hriday aims to make the meeting place between death and life more tolerable for those human beings neglected by society. The sisters show the dying that they are valued and respected. They interpret death as "finding God again," not as a critical opportunity for conversion. As missionaries, the sisters give testimony to their faith simply through what they do: love. They respect the beliefs—and the unbeliefs—of all those who come there. For example, the sisters will sprinkle the dying Hindu with water from the Ganges River, read a passage from the Koran to the dying Moslem, and observe the appropriate rites of death with the Christian.

Although Mother Teresa cared little for keeping records of her activities, primarily because keeping records took time that was better spent meeting the needs of the poor, all deaths that have occurred at Nirmal Hriday since its opening more than forty years ago are recorded in a register. By following the requirements of the law, the sisters have shown their respect and good intentions.

Today, Nirmal Hriday stands as a monument to human life, even when that life is barely perceptible in its final heartbeat. It has become the best-known site associated with Mother Teresa and the Missionaries of Charity. In fact, Calcutta officials include it in the city's official guidebooks, not because they admire it but because they consider it a tourist attraction. To go to Calcutta and not visit Kalighat to see the product of Mother Teresa's work is like going to Rome and failing to see the Vatican. Kalighat, however, offers more than tourist interest; it contains the passion and love of hearts acting on the impulse of a message that renews itself every day.

So strong is the charism of Nirmal Hriday that many individuals and groups volunteer their services to work there. Some volunteers are medical students from the West who work at Nirmal Hriday as part of their educational training. Others are professionals who simply take a year's sabbatical to help the sisters. Many volunteers, after a month's stay in Nirmal Hriday, assert that they have never known a happier time. Exposure to Mother Teresa's work often prompts young volunteers to embrace the way of life of the sisters. Many Missionaries of Charity around the world found their initial calling confirmed in the atmosphere of love and compassion in Nirmal Hriday.[3]

THE SPREAD OF LOVE

Mother Teresa's service on behalf of the poor actually began with the children in Calcutta's outlying district of Motijhil, the slum near the high school where she had taught for eighteen years. The rigid cloister life of the Sisters of Loreto had scarcely allowed her the opportunity to visit the area. Although her students frequently mentioned the slums, she never knew exactly where they were located.

As she took her initial steps into total service to the poor, Mother Teresa asked Father Henry, "Could you tell me where the neighborhood of Motijhil is?"

"How's that, Sister?" Father responded. "Don't tell me you don't know. It's right next door to the high school and convent where you have lived all these years."

Coincidental? Providential? It didn't matter to Mother

Teresa. She found the heart of the slums and began her work: teaching. First, she offered basic and elementary lessons in hygiene. On the first day, five children showed up; on the second day, twenty-one more arrived. Within a few days more than fifty children clustered for Mother Teresa's rudimentary curriculum.

Classes were held outdoors on a bare patch of earth under a tree. Into her simple lessons on personal hygiene, Mother Teresa gradually integrated instructions on manners, matters of faith, math, and reading. With a generous donation, which did not get channeled immediately into some other worthy cause, Mother Teresa rented a shack and purchased a blackboard. The children were then sheltered from the sun and rain, and classes could continue with greater regularity.

As she developed her small system of public education, several details came to Mother Teresa's attention. First, she learned that she was not the only one "teaching" the children. Others, far less charitable, were teaching the children to steal and keeping the "goods" for themselves. After Nirmal Hriday was established, she also learned that many of the dying feared for the well-being of their children who would be left abandoned in the streets.

In her faithful observation of heavenly signs, Mother Teresa understood that God was asking her to respond in love. She saw in her students, and in the countless children who remained far from her sight, the goodness of her beloved Jesus. With tenacity and faith, she set about plans to acquire a building and surrounding acreage—located on the same street as the motherhouse—to use for the care of these children. In time, Mother Teresa's compassion for needy children would extend far beyond the immediate neighborhood of the Missionaries of Charity motherhouse. Today, in addition to Shishu Bhavan, the center near the motherhouse, the Missionaries of Charity operate several such centers in Delhi, Darjeeling, Rome, Florence (Italy), and Setúbal (Portugal).[4] Among these is Nirmala Kennedy Center, located in the zone of Dum Dum in Calcutta, not far from the airport. The family of the late Joseph Kennedy, Jr., sponsors the Missionaries of Charity in their mission at this center.

∽

As Mother Teresa's small community grew to number more than fifty sisters, she began to spread the love of God even farther.[5] Especially needy among the Calcutta population were the people with leprosy.

To enable the Missionaries of Charity to reach these outcasts of society, Mother Teresa exercised an initiative of creativity and compassion: she started her so-called "mobile clinics." Mother Teresa avoided, if at all possible, having any office or headquarters building; she embraced simplicity as part of her solidarity with the poor.[6] A highly structured approach to healthcare would require money and energy that could be better directed toward meeting the most pressing needs of the poor; thus, she devised the "mobile clinics." They were no more than a few sisters carrying their small medicine kits and traveling by public transportation into the areas where the needs of people with leprosy were critical.

With time, Mother Teresa was able to establish centers that ministered to the specific needs of people with leprosy. One center, established in Asansol, India, during the early sixties, was constructed with the money collected from the public raffle of the limousine given to Mother Teresa by Pope Paul VI when he visited India in 1964 for the International Eucharistic Congress. Nearly twenty years later, in 1980, Mother Teresa used the money from the Nobel Prize for Peace to construct a self-governing village in Titagarh, India, for the rehabilitation of people with leprosy.

THE CO-WORKERS

The Co-Workers of Mother Teresa existed among the sick and the suffering long before the group had an official identity. Mother Teresa called them her "treasure chest." Despite the fact that their numbers were few, the Co-Workers drew a great deal of support and confidence from Mother Teresa. Impeded physically from serving the poor, Co-Workers gave support to the active service of the sisters by offering God their prayers and sufferings, with each Co-Worker prayerfully supporting an individual missionary.[7] Later, a group of contemplative Co-Workers was established; they were distinguished from the earlier Co-Workers by their commitment (spiritual twinning) to a particular community of the Missionaries of Charity.

In 1954 a group of active Co-Workers, destined to be the largest, was established. The first of these Co-Workers was Ann Blaikie, the Englishwoman who "caught" a passion and spirit for the poor that would fashion her as a supporter of Mother Teresa for the rest of her life. Supporting Mother Teresa's work in the United States was Violet Collins, who with her husband became an active spokesperson in Washington, D.C., for the International Association of Co-Workers of Mother Teresa. In the eighties, the active Co-Workers diversified organizationally into youth Co-Workers, health Co-Workers, and Co-Worker priests.

The Co-Workers were dedicated and tireless. Among Mother Teresa's early Co-Workers were Charu Ma, a cook from the school of the Sisters of Loreto who had great affection for Mother Teresa; Michael Gomes, Mother Teresa's generous "landlord" at Greek Lane 14; and Michael Gomes' family. Especially in her first years after leaving the Sisters of Loreto, Mother Teresa relied on the kindness and generosity of these people to help her take those first uncertain steps toward fulfilling her mission.

Although most religious orders look to their third orders to provide support by influencing society, there is no evidence that Mother Teresa had planned to create a lay movement to assist the Missionaries of Charity. As the organization of Co-Workers providentially evolved, Mother Teresa shifted her philosophy regarding its mission. Originally, she encouraged her Co-Workers to collect money and articles for the poor. She reversed her thinking, however, and chose to prohibit any type of begging. Instead of expecting her Co-Workers to provide material substance from any source, she wanted them to give, first and foremost, of their own treasures: love and mercy.

～

Rarely do female congregations give birth to male congregations. In fact, canon law prohibits—as it did when the Missionaries of Charity Brothers were born—a female from serving as the head of a community of religious men. Although such an evolution was not unprecedented in the Catholic Church, Mother Teresa never anticipated that her Missionaries of Charity would eventually include a male component. But in 1963, when several men—biological brothers of Missionaries of Charity—conveyed to her a desire to dedicate their lives as their sisters had, Mother Teresa responded to the will of God.

Because of the numerous and agonizing tasks related to the Missionaries of Charity that she already shouldered, Mother Teresa would have been thoroughly justified in retreating from or neglecting the new congregation of men. But she didn't retreat; she was convinced that God would not introduce her to something that he was not going to give her the strength and wisdom to handle. She put her heart and her hands to the task—without breaking Church laws, without "unclothing one saint in order to clothe another," and without neglecting to pay attention to the needs of the young and struggling Congregation of the Missionaries of Charity.

Whereas plans for a women's congregation had been risky, plans for a male congregation were more so. Without having obtained approval for the first institute, Mother Teresa was setting up another, against which prejudices were even greater. First, she was venturing into a male world, and at that time, of course, Mother Teresa didn't enjoy the ecclesiastical "clout" she would have years later. Second, previous similar attempts in mission territory had failed.

"One needs to push oneself to the core," Mother Teresa commented, "as if all depended on oneself, and then have the greatest confidence, as if all depended on God." With that confident faith, she brought together the core of the institute of brothers, offered directions similar to those followed by the Missionaries of Charity, and proposed that a priest, possibly a Jesuit, be the spiritual leader of the group in formation.

She spoke with various priests, but not one was able to comply with her request. The priests, good people all of them, assured her that although they appreciated her offer, none believed they had the charism of a "cofounder."

If not for her "Slavic stubbornness," which perhaps could be more accurately interpreted as strength of faith and character, Mother Teresa might have given up her efforts to establish a male congregation, but her tenacity had its rewards.

In March 1963 Father Ian Travers-Ball, an Australian Jesuit and missionary in India, heard about the existence of a group of young men who had vowed to serve the poor in a spirit similar to that of the Missionaries of Charity. The young priest knew of Mother Teresa and her work and chose to participate in a month-long experiment that involved working closely with her. At the end of that month, Mother Teresa asked Father Travers if he would agree to take charge of the young men and direct their formation.

Father Travers postponed his response; he wanted time to think and pray, and he needed to discuss the situation with his superiors. He was given two options: to continue to be a Jesuit, serving at the head of these young men as his gifts were needed, or to renounce being a Jesuit and become a Missionary of Charity brother. Father Travers became Brother Andrew and assumed the title of general servant, head of the Missionaries of Charity Brothers.

While Brother Andrew put to use his Jesuit formation, optimism, and capacity for amiable leadership, Mother Teresa relaxed her attention to the newly formed brothers. Results were soon evident. The brothers developed a clear spiritual identification, and their numbers increased. In a spirit that incorporated Ignatian ingredients into Mother Teresa's mold, the brothers spread from India to Africa, America, and Europe.

Brother Andrew remained at the front of the Missionaries of Charity Brothers until 1988. He was succeeded by Brother Geof, a fellow Australian who dedicated his canonical mandate to consolidating the formation of the brothers and to bringing discipline to their rapid growth around the world.

Ian Travers-Ball—Brother Andrew—knew that an important part of his life had come to a close. He felt privileged to have been a coparticipant in the charism of Mother Teresa.

Mother Teresa is determined to bring natural family planning within reach of the poorest Indian. Spring 1974. *(CNS Photo)*

Mother Teresa comforts a twenty-eight-year-old Bengali man at Kalighat, home for the sick and dying. *(Photo by Steve Kemperman)*

A crowded Calcutta street.
(Photo by Steve Kemperman)

Mother Teresa consults with one of her
Missionaries of Charity at her home of the destitute and dying in
Calcutta, October 18, 1979. *(CNS Photo)*

Holding a rosary, Mother Teresa tells a Denver audience, "Do small things with great love." *(CNS Photo by James Baca)*

A Bengali man receives a bath at Kalighat.

(Photo by Steve Kemperman)

Mother Teresa greets a young disabled person at the Youth Corps-sponsored Jesus and Global Peace Rally held at Varsity Stadium in Toronto, Canada, June 27, 1982. *(Photo by Bill Wittman)*

Mother Teresa's visit with President and Mrs. Reagan.
(CNS Photo)

Mother Teresa shares an informal moment with
fifteen nuns before making their final vows at St. Aloysius Church in
N.W. Washington, June 1995. *(CNS Photo by Michael Alexander)*

Mother Teresa responding to the enthusiasm and hope
of the crowd at the Jesus and Global Peace Rally, Varsity Stadium,
Toronto, Canada, June 27, 1982. *(Photo by Bill Wittman)*

Mother Teresa bows her head during a prayer service at Charlotte Coliseum in Charlotte, North Carolina, where she spoke to a crowd of about 13,000 people, June 14, 1995. *(CNS Photo by Donna Jernigan)*

Part III

~

A LEGACY
OF LOVE

Chapter 5

A PLATFORM FOR LIFE

Mother Teresa insisted that she and her sisters were not interested in and did not participate in conventional politics. Yet, by cultural standards, Mother Teresa was very much "involved" in politics—the politics of justice and compassion for all people.

As an international figure, advocating on behalf of marginalized people everywhere, Mother Teresa could not avoid the political arena. As a prophet of peace, she spoke for the weakest amid the strongest; she spoke clarity and truth to those who hid behind convoluted words and shrouded promises. When asked what advice she would give to politicians, she hesitated, insisting that she did not give advice to professionals. But she offered her concern that politicians probably don't spend much time on their knees. If politicians prayed a little more, she offered, they surely would recognize the pain and injustice within their own systems.

Mother Teresa herself spent more than half her life in prayer, and from that stance of praise, she could easily perceive the needs of others. She did not merely "help" the poor; she *loved* them—which was to make her a committed and effective politician. She was a genuine "civil servant," serving others in their daily struggle for survival, not on paper or in chambers far from the streets.

AN ADVOCATE FOR THE FAMILY

Mother Teresa's testimony was always clear and noble; her intentions were driven by love, not by a self-constructed and self-centered political image. She never wanted to force her convictions on others or create an authoritarian movement camouflaged as religiosity. Perhaps for that very reason, she was a powerful advocate to be reckoned with in any discussion about a controversial issue.

Mother Teresa considered the family unit a sacred creation. "Love begins at home," she never ceased to teach. "Peace begins with a smile. Holiness is not a luxury for a few, but a simple duty for all of us. We must all be holy, you and I. Works of love are works of peace. What I can do, you cannot do; what you can do, I cannot do. But together, you and I can do something beautiful for God."

Abortion: On behalf of the family, Mother Teresa was tenaciously outspoken against abortion. When she appeared before an audience as a guest speaker, she invariably weaved in comments about abortion as a crime against children, women, and life. For her, life was something coming forth from the kind and generous hand of God; thus, she used every opportunity to teach others to respect the ultimate gift of new life. When she accepted the Nobel Prize for Peace, for example, Mother Teresa did not hesitate to insist that abortion is the greatest of crimes. There, in the presence of representatives from many countries that allowed abortion, she spoke with conviction, courage, and truth.

So powerful a defender of life was Mother Teresa that, upon invitations from representatives of the Catholic Church hierarchy, she consented to take part in marches and demonstrations against abortion in Spain and Italy when their respective parliaments were debating the legalization of abortion. On May 13, 1981, the day an attempt was made on John Paul II's life in Saint Peter's Square, Mother Teresa marched in Florence against a referendum on abortion. That night, she was scheduled to deliver an address against the referendum, but the circumstances of the day suggested a change in the program. After Cardinal Giovanni Benelli led the audience in a sung Mass in the Church of Bellariva, Mother Teresa offered this reflection:

> Let us pray for the Holy Father, but let us make a promise: in this most beautiful city of Florence, we cannot permit that any child be condemned to die in the womb of its mother....If you are afraid of the child, turn it over to me. I will take care of him and God will not let him lack anything. Let us offer this Holy Mass for the Holy Father and for all the mothers who are afraid of their as-yet-unborn child. And let us ask Our Lady that she help us to love all children, born and not yet born, just as she loved Jesus. Let us learn from the poor. The poor person never will commit abortion. It is possible that she may abandon her child, but she will never kill him or her. The country which is afraid of its children is a poor country, the poorest of all countries.

Recalling this incident, Florentine Co-Worker Mario Bertini adds:

> Things then unfolded in the way that we all know. Proposition 194, with the backing of the referendum, institutionalized abortion, and Mother Teresa, faithful to her promise, returned to Florence to open a house whose objective is to help all the mothers who have difficulties so that they do not see themselves tempted to deprive themselves of the child which is about to be born.

Although Mother Teresa's presence and principles were not enough to keep abortion regulations from passing their respective lawmaking bodies, she by no means ceased her plea for life. For her, life comes directly from the hand of God, and this fact was never far from her central message. Discussion among biologists about the moment in which life begins or among theologians about when the human soul enters the fetus were too academic and abstract for her. She wanted only to live her convictions. She loved the Christ that agonizes in the dying, the deprived, the poor, the aborted child. When she reached into the trash to cradle a dying fetus in her hands—the tiny human heart barely throbbing with a whisper of life—she spoke volumes about the value of human life and how that precious value cannot be disregarded, no matter how minimal it might seem.

It is amazing to review the amount of press coverage that Mother Teresa generated without a staff of campaign managers and copywriters. For example, among the pieces that constitute a magazine article library dedicated specifically to articles about Mother Teresa, there are two clippings from the London Catholic daily, *The Universe*, dated April 15 and April 20, 1988. Those dates marked the celebration of a conference on earth resources, held in Oxford and attended by ninety religious leaders (including the archbishop of Canterbury, the Dalai Lama, and the cardinal-archbishop of Vienna, Franz König) and seventy political leaders. Understandably, the organizers had invited Mother Teresa of Calcutta.

In the concise style of a journalistic headline, the clipping from *The Universe* for April 15 alluded to "Mother Teresa's Shock at Britain's Homeless," indicating her surprise and distress at the number of people lacking shelter in Great Britain. The London daily documented its article with a photograph of Mother Teresa and Cardinal Primate Basil Hume, caught by surprise during the night in their search for the poor in the district of Lincoln's Inn Fields. The article included the following quote from Mother Teresa:

> It is surprising to observe that there are many other rich countries, such as this one, where there is so little care for others. To make sure that this class of persons feels loved, wanted, and cared for is a very beautiful work. Jesus is present in every disfigured face.

The second clipping from *The Universe* five days later touts another impressive headline: "Match for Maggie." The article is accompanied by a photograph of Mother Teresa and Deputy David Alton, a Catholic and sponsor of a proposal for amending the law on abortion that would reduce the period when a woman could have an abortion to the first eighteen weeks of gestation.

Mother Teresa took advantage of her stay in London to ask

to meet with then Prime Minister Margaret Thatcher. She wanted to call the attention of the Iron Lady to the condition of the homeless and to support the amendment to the abortion law.

Before arriving at Number Ten Downing Street, however, Mother Teresa expressed her disagreement respecting the limit of eighteen weeks proposed by Deputy Alton:

> Abortion is not legitimate, even within a week. Abortion is a double murder: of the child and of the conscience of the mother. Mrs. Thatcher is a mother. I think she will understand. Every child, including the handicapped, is a gift of God. If someone does not want a child, let her give the child to me. I will look for a family to adopt it.

A month later, June 17, 1988, *The Universe* published another article on abortion, under the headline "Jail Abortion Doctors." The headline captured the essence of Mother Teresa's antiabortionist message on the occasion of a tour through the United States and Mexico:

> Mother Teresa stated in America that she would like to jail doctors who perform abortions. She also said that abortion is double murder—the killing of an unborn child and of a woman's conscience. During her visit to the United States and Mexico, Mother Teresa spoke to students, prisoners, and the poor. In Saint Louis, she said: "If I had the power, I would open a jail and would put every single doctor who performs abortions in jail for killing a child—the gift of God." Speaking on behalf of pro-life groups,

she said that abortion "has become the greatest de-
stroyer of love and peace."

The dignity of women: Mother Teresa's conviction about the
sacred value of the family motivated her to accept an invitation to participate in world conferences on the family held by
Catholic organizations in France (Paray-le-Monial, July 1985),
Spain (Madrid, September 1987), and England (Brighton, July,
1990). Before renowned specialists, Mother Teresa repeated
her simple, practical, and highly intelligible concepts about
the primacy of love, the capacity of prayer for uniting the family, and a mother's role in the bosom of the family.

Needless to say, Mother Teresa's apparent traditional stance
on these and other themes often disappointed those not familiar with her beliefs. For example, she had participated, as
the Vatican's delegate, in an international conference on women
celebrated in Mexico during the early seventies. The conference's platform had a clear vindictive character, and the tone
of Mother Teresa's presentation starkly clashed with the expectations of the banner carriers of feminism. She made the
following comment to Belgian Jesuit Father Edward Le Joly
about the conference:

> It was disagreeable. No one talked about God. Well,
> it's possible that someone did, but I did not hear it.
> For my part, I spoke about the dignity of woman,
> of the functions and prerogatives which God has
> confided to her. Insofar as being mother and wife,
> they are called to be the very center of the home, to
> turn it into a happy home for her husband and chil-
> dren. It is a very noble vocation, that of mothers of

the human race. I told them that they had the privi-
lege of giving generously, in the same way in which
God has given to his children (Quoted in *Servant of
Love: Mother Teresa and her Missionaries of Charity*,
Harper & Row, San Francisco, 1977, p. 10).

Humanitarian efforts: John Paul II, and Paul VI before him,
frequently relied on Mother Teresa to carry out delicate missions concerning humanitarian tasks, including those that involved political situations. These missions were confided to
her as a last resort, knowing that she was the only person who
could remain truly neutral and who had enough credibility to
be accepted without suspicion by all parties and political entities involved. The missions were always riddled with tension
and potential danger. If it hadn't been for Mother Teresa's temperament—her interior serenity and her faith—she would have
been worn down by the stress.[1]

Unfortunately, Mother Teresa's missions did not always have
the desired success, at least not immediately. For example, me-
diation with traditionalist Archbishop Marcel Lefebvre was
confided to her, without success. According to a credible source,
Mother Teresa wrote five letters to the archbishop but did not
receive a reply to any of them.

Mother Teresa was asked to meet with Reverend Ian Pais-
ley, the religious leader of Northern Ireland, but was also un-
successful here. She failed, too, when she was asked to inter-
vene with the Ayatollah Khomeini on behalf of the families of
the American embassy personnel held in Iran in December
1979. The request for intervention reached her when she was
returning from Oslo, Norway, where she had just received the
Nobel Prize for Peace. She went to the Iranian embassy and

confessed to the ambassador: "I don't know anything. I have been too busy to read the newspapers. I come to Your Excellency with the same feelings as those of a mother who sighs for her children. They have asked me to do so. I am ready to go to Iran or to speak by telephone with the Ayatollah." The ambassador promised her he would look into the subject. If indeed he did, his interest did not produce good results.

A VOICE AMONG NATIONS

History will record the details of Mother Teresa's participation in world politics. The human heart, however, needs no such documentation to realize that a powerful goodness has passed this way.

The moment of greatest political significance for Mother Teresa, the day when she "ascended" to the most important and representative forum of world politics, was October 26, 1985.

It was the final day of the week commemorating the fortieth anniversary of the foundation of the United Nations. Throughout the previous days, kings, heads of state, prime ministers, and diplomats of the most important countries in the world had filed past the dias. The closing event, however, was a unique and historic moment for the United Nations: a Catholic nun spoke to the world's political elite.

Perhaps Mother Teresa felt the weight of her surroundings, but the pressure did not influence the content of her message. She spoke, as she had spoken in Oslo, Milan, Florence, Pescara (Italy), Sulmona (Italy), Bologna, Tokyo, Paris, Atlanta, Brussels, Hamburg, Melbourne, and elsewhere, about the poorest of the poor as the image of God, about abortion as a double crime, and about peace as the fruit of love among people.

Secretary-General Javier Pérez de Cuéllar introduced Mother Teresa as "the most powerful woman on earth":

> We are in a hall of words. In past days there have filed by this podium the supposedly most powerful men in the world. Today the opportunity offers itself to us of welcoming the presence of truly the most powerful woman on earth. I don't believe there is any necessity for introducing her. She does not ask for words; she asks for deeds. I am convinced that the best thing I could do is render her homage and tell her that she is much more important than I am or than all of us are. She is the United Nations! She is the peace of the world!

Mother Teresa was not particularly impressed with the secretary-general's words, but she accepted them with gratitude as an unmerited gesture of generosity on the part of the Peruvian diplomat, who was decidedly moved with respect. She quickly moved to focus on her own purpose for being there:

> We ought to give thanks to God that during forty years he has permitted the United Nations to develop its activity for the good of all the people on earth. We are all children of God. No difference of color, of nationality, or of race ought to separate us....Today we live very affected by the threat of nuclear war, we flee the thought of AIDS, but we do not hinder unborn children from being killed. Abortion is a great destroyer of peace. When we eliminate an unborn child, we are trying to eliminate God.

Among those invited to the event was Cardinal John J. O'Connor, archbishop of New York. Some days later, he wrote a column in *Catholic New York* in which he coined Pérez de Cuéllar's description of Mother Teresa: "the most powerful woman."

> The secretary general of the United Nations described as *the most powerful woman* that little stooped over woman whom we know as Mother Teresa of Calcutta....Mother Teresa had not come to the United Nations to speak, but to be present for the showing of an excellent documentary about her life, produced by two sisters, Ann and Jeannette Petrie. At the end of the documentary she agreed to say some words, while several hundred important personalities tried to dry their tears without being observed. Her first words were right on the mark, but they seemed somewhat ironical for those who still remember the East-West dispute on the occasion of the inauguration of the United Nations forty years ago. The dispute was over whether the sessions should begin with a prayer or not. The West ended up losing. Last Saturday afternoon, October 26, forty years later, Mother Teresa asked all those who packed the hall of the General Assembly that they read with her a prayer for peace. From where I was situated, I could not observe everyone, but by the echo of voices it seemed clear that not very many could have abstained from complying with her request.

In addition to public invitations to participate in the political arena, Mother Teresa was known to take the initiative when she felt that critical issues of justice were at stake. The attitude that led her to send a harsh letter, dated March 26, 1979, to Indian Prime Minister Morarji Desai was seemingly more political than any other attitude she displayed.

This unusual action was Mother Teresa's response to a proposal for a law titled "On Religious Liberty," which was not adopted and appears, in fact, to have been decisive in the defeat of Desai.

This proposed law, under the guise of wanting to avoid conversions promoted by force, trickery, or bribery, constituted an underhanded attack on the work of the Missionaries of Charity and attributed to them attempts at Catholic proselytism in their centers for children and the dying. This situation led Mother Teresa to take the exceptional step— for her—of writing a letter to the prime minister. The letter read:

> I fear, Mister Prime Minister, that you are falling short of fulfilling what you swore in the name of God to do when you took office. I fear for my people. You have authorized abortion, an act that is sowing hatred in our country because, if a mother can kill her child, why are we not going to be able to kill others, those who get in our way?...What explanation will you be able to give, on the day that you meet God face to face, for the destruction of life of so many innocent unborn children?...Religion is not something over which you or I can dictate laws. Religion implies adoration of God. It is, for that

reason, a matter of conscience, in which each one is called to decide what he wishes to do.

In my case, the religion which I live and practice is Catholicism. It constitutes my life, my joy, and the greatest proof of the love which God has for me. But no one can deny that I love my people very much, that I love them more than myself, and that, logically, I would want to share with them the joy of this treasure. That does not depend upon me, nor am I able to force on anyone that he or she accept my religion.

In the same way, neither can any man, law, or government demand that anyone reject a religion which promises him or her peace, joy, love....The father of our country, Gandhi, said: "He who serves the poor, serves God." I spend hours and hours helping the poor and dying, the marginalized, despised human beings, lepers, the physically and psychologically incapacitated, because I love God and I know that all that I do for my brothers and sisters, the poor, I do for him. This is the only motive and joy for my life: to love and serve God in the poor, in those who are hungry or thirsty, in those who are naked, in those who have no home.

Mr. Desai and members of Parliament: in the name of this God, whom some of you call Ishwar and others Allah, do not destroy our people's liberty to love and serve God in keeping with one's conscience and one's beliefs. Do not minimize the Hindu religion by saying that the Hindu people sell their faith for a plate of rice. Never have I seen—

and my experience is great now—such a thing happen, in spite of our giving food daily to thousands of needy persons of every religion and caste, and thousands of them have died in our arms, happy in the peace of the God in whom they believed.

Mother Teresa also took the initiative to influence presidents of the United States on behalf of the poor around the world. For example, In the first months of 1981, Mother Teresa sent a letter to President Ronald Reagan on behalf of the victims of the widespread drought in Ethiopia. A few days after receiving the request from Mother Teresa, President Reagan called her and offered an account of how he had organized and launched a massive assistance plan.

Mother Teresa also wrote to President George Bush and to Iraq's Saddam Hussein (January 2, 1991) in the hope of dissuading them from going to war. Although her letters didn't have the desired results, the political entities involved continued to respect Mother Teresa and the remarkable measures of humanitarian dignity that she could generate. Her appeal embodies the timeless message of peace that will echo around the world for generations to come:

I write to you with tears in my eyes and with the love of God in my heart, to beg you on behalf of the poor and on behalf of those who will end up being poor in the event that the war which threatens us is unchained. I beg you with all my heart that you spare no efforts in favor of the peace of God and to reconcile yourselves with one another.

Each one of you has concerns enough and citizens enough to keep you busy, but first begin by hearing the One who came to the world to teach us peace. You have the capacity and force to destroy the presence and image of God, in his men, in his women, and in his children. Listen, please, to the voice of God. God has created us to love each other with his love and not to destroy ourselves with our hates.

In a short while it could be that there'll be victors and vanquished in this war which threatens all of us, but which can never justify the suffering, pain, and losses of life which your canons will produce.

I speak to you in the name of God, that God whom we all love and share, in order to beg you on behalf of the innocents, our poor of the world, and those who will become poor because of the war. It is they who will suffer the most, not being able to hide themselves. I beg you for them on my knees. They will have to suffer, and when that occurs, we will be the ones guilty of not having done all that is possible to protect them and love them. I beg you on behalf of those who will become orphans or widows, and who will suffer loneliness because their parents, their husbands, their brothers, and their children will have perished.

I beg you: do not deprive them of their lives. I beg you on behalf of those who will become handicapped and disfigured. They are children of God. I beg you on behalf of those who will end up without home, without food, without love. Think of them as if they were your own children.

I beg you, finally, on behalf of those who will be deprived of the most precious gift which God is able to give us: life. I beg you that you save our brothers and sisters, yours and ours, because God gives them to us to love them and to care for them. We do not have the right to destroy what God has given us. Please, please: allow your intelligence to be the intelligence and will of God. You have the capacity to bring war into the world and to make peace. Please, choose the way of peace.

I, my Sisters, and our poor do not fail to pray intensely for you. The whole world is united in prayer that you open your hearts to the love of God. You might win the war, but what will be the cost to those who will find themselves broken, mutilated, displaced?

I appeal to you: to your love, to your love of God, and of your neighbors. In the name of God and of those whom you are going to condemn to poverty, do not destroy life and peace. Let love and peace triumph and let your names be recorded for the good you have done, the joy you have sown, and the love you have shared.

Pray for me and for my Sisters who try to love and serve the poor because they are the beloved possession of God. In the same way, we and our poor pray for you. We pray that you love and care for that which God has confided to your care with such love.

May God bless you today and always.

AN IMAGE OF POWER

The world has captured the power of Mother Teresa in photography, in the printed word, and in national and personal memory: a legacy of power. With a single-minded purpose, Mother Teresa placed her image—her entire person and life—at the service of the poor. To bring her message to as many people as possible, she would allow journalists to photograph her with leading world figures. She posed for a photo with Imelda Marcos of Manila before the latter was exiled. Later, she was photographed with President Corazón Aquino. She was photographed with the wife of François Duvalier, Haiti's president; with Princess Diana of Wales; with President Ronald Reagan; with singers Albano and Romina Power; with the leader of the Palestinian Liberation Organization, Yassir Arafāt; with Venezuelan Presidents Luis Herrera Campins and Carlos Andrés Pérez Rodríguez; with Mexican President Luis Echeverría Alvarez; with English Prime Minister Margaret Thatcher; with Queen Elizabeth II; with Ethiopian Emperor Haile Selassie; with Roberto Mesa, the general who led a coup in Bolivia.

Mother Teresa has let herself be photographed in the company of the rich and famous in the hope that her own efforts on behalf of the poor would be ultimately served. She never considered "selling" her photo rights to anyone, nor did her availability for photographs imply approval of certain human attitudes and/or politics, which in some cases were reproachable. With constant faith, Mother Teresa simply turned her photographic popularity into prayer by offering it for the souls in purgatory. She affirmed more than once that, for each photograph taken, she asked God to free a soul from purgatory.

The printed word, too, captured her power. Pérez de Cuéllar's phrase, used in his introductory comments at the United Nations, describing Mother Teresa as "the most powerful woman on earth," became the title for news articles, commentaries, and chapters in biographies about her. But hers was a power unlike the power that the world understands and covets. Mother Teresa's power was more authentic and profound— a power that was not based on the force of ready military might, terrorist threats, or economic sanctions. Her power was the authority inherent in gentleness, derived from the conviction that to do good is beautiful and gratifying from both the eschatological perspective and the perspective of the here and now. Hers was a power that had tremendous force simply because she exercised it exclusively for the benefit of the weakest and the poorest.

Was Mother Teresa conscious of this power? On one occasion, someone asked her, half in jest, "Are you aware, Mother Teresa, of what they say about you, that you are the most powerful woman in the world?"

She answered, "I wish it were true. I would use my powers to banish wars from the world."

Chapter 6

PARABLES OF LOVE

A book of excellent religious literature, although better known in Italy than elsewhere, is titled *The Little Flowers of Saint Francis of Assisi*. One of the "little flowers" of the *Poverello* refers to an occasion when Francis invited one of his followers to go with him to preach. After Francis and his companion—cloaked in their hooded habits, with hands in the cuffs of the opposite sleeve, in an attitude of reflection—had made two trips through the streets of Assisi, Francis announced, "Brother, we're finished. Now we've done our preaching." Having done nothing more than take a brief walk in the silent presence of God, the two returned to the friary. The companion expressed his astonishment and asked Francis how their preaching could possibly be finished when they encountered no one and approached no one along their walk. "Brother," Francis answered, "we have preached with our example."

Although Francis's invitation to his brother to take a preaching walk through the streets of Assisi is a scenario out of medieval times, the anecdote has the touch of a parable. It would have never occurred to Mother Teresa to walk around in the same manner; she was far more sensible and pragmatic. In her service to the poorest of the poor of Christ, however, she did her share of walking at a good pace hundreds of times, not on peaceful streets like those of ancient Assisi but on the busy streets of the whole world, and she has left countless parables that teach the power of love. Such was the nature of her teaching by example—accomplished with few, if any, words at all. Her sisters continue to live what she taught through their examples of love demonstrated in cities remote from India, where their white-and-blue saris and their simple sandals worn without socks attract attention.

Nothing can better demonstrate Mother Teresa's teaching authority than the countless stories—the parables—that capture her in the act of love.

~

Mother Teresa's first visit to Spain took place June 6, 1976. She arrived by plane from New York, where she had visited the houses of the congregation in the United States. The journey was her response to an invitation by then Archbishop Cardinal Tarancón of Madrid, who had asked her to open a house in his diocese. Mother Teresa's immediate objective, however, wasn't to open a house; as usual, she wanted to see for herself the social conditions of the marginalized population that her congregation would serve.

The trip probably would have gone better if Mother Teresa herself had presented her Indian passport to the customs police. Instead, a steward of Iberia Airlines, one of the few Spaniards who knew about Mother Teresa, offered to do it for her.

The steward was dumbfounded when he heard the customs

police say that, with an Indian passport and without a visa, the owner of the passport could not enter the country. Trying to reason with the customs official, the steward suggested that surely an exception could be made for someone like Mother Teresa of Calcutta. He was even further surprised that none of the customs police had any idea who Mother Teresa was.

With every good intention of explaining to the official who Mother Teresa was, the steward offered certain inaccurate statements. For example, he said that Mother Teresa was the most important nun in the world, that she had received many prizes, that the pope valued her very much, and that she had come on the invitation of the most eminent Cardinal Tarancón to open a large center for the poor. The steward was not convincing.

"As you must understand," the customs official insisted, "we have rules that we must adhere to. Nevertheless, we will telephone headquarters to see if they will authorize an exception. The law is the law, no matter how important, in your understanding, this nun is."

The telephone call took fifteen minutes. Meanwhile, the expressions on people's faces told Mother Teresa that something strange must be happening. When she found out exactly what the problem was, she took her Vatican diplomatic passport out of her cloth bag. She used this document, given to her by Pope Paul VI for those missions in which her Indian nationality would be a liability, only when absolutely necessary.

She discreetly placed the passport back in her bag when the chief of the police detachment at the Madrid airport returned with good news. Mother Teresa could stay in the country for seventy-two hours without a visa.

Humbly thanking the man, but declining his generous permission, she said that her schedule called for her to leave for Rome the following morning. The chief of police, won over by the woman's apparent simplicity, proceeded to greet Mother Teresa personally and to wish her a pleasant stay in Madrid. Then, when he chanced to find out about her Vatican passport, he lamented: "It's a shame they did not tell me about it before. With a document like that, they would have opened all the doors to you, without having to ask for any special authorization."

⌒

The original core of Co-Workers in Spain hoped that Mother Teresa would be pleased about the bank account they had opened in her name. The money had come from good people who wanted to support her efforts even before she acquired her first house there. Mother Teresa accepted the money because she respected the good intentions of those who had generously offered it for her poor. She told the sisters, however, that if people gave money spontaneously, it could be accepted and faithfully directed to the purposes for which the donors intended it, but she wanted none of them ever to ask for money or anything else. Money was not the most important thing; rather, generous and joyful service on the part of each one toward the poorest of the poor was paramount.

As donations continued to accumulate in the bank account, the account number was somehow divulged, as well as the address of the Co-Workers. On one occasion, a check for two thousand dollars arrived from a Puerto Rico benefactor. A Co-Worker, in Rome on the same date that Mother Teresa was there, took the opportunity to present the check to her personally.

While Mother Teresa attended the religious profession of several novices in the chapel of the Missionaries of Charity in San Gregorio al Celio, the two-thousand-dollar check disappeared from the table where it had been left. Although she seemed to experience a moment of discomfort, Mother Teresa recovered her calm after putting herself in the shoes of the thief. When someone suggested notifying the police, Mother Teresa responded: "All in all, the dollars had been donated to the poor. If it so happens that he knows how to administer this money with good judgment, the poor beggar will be able to cover his basic necessities for a little while. May God help him."

⤳

October 17, 1979, witnessed an event that perhaps remains the best known to the public in the life of Mother Teresa. The news spread around the world instantly by radio, print, and television: Mother Teresa of Calcutta had won the Nobel Prize for Peace. Millions of people who knew little, if anything at all, about the woman's work learned of her existence and extraordinary character. So extraordinary was the woman that the most demanding committee of a country as distant from India—and from Rome—as Norway, with absolutely no religious criteria, set itself in a human-social-religious trajectory to declare her worthy of the most prestigious prize in the world.

Although the exact number of votes is kept secret, Mother Teresa had to receive at least the majority of committee votes. What did become public, with expressions as varied as they were unequivocal, was the unanimous applause in the surrounding "global village" from those who had knowledge of her work. All agreed that her labor had made her so worthy of the prize that, in reality, the one receiving the prize gave honor to the prize, rather than the prize giving honor to the one receiving it.

The designation of Mother Teresa as the Nobel winner for 1979 reflected well on the institution that granted the award. Throughout the decade of the seventies, there had been a great deal of criticism about the political nature that the prize seemed to be acquiring. Awarding it to Chancellor Willy Brandt, for example, for his *ostpolitik*, was criticized in 1971. Giving the prize jointly to U.S. Secretary of State Henry Kissinger and North Vietnam Prime Minister Le Duc Tho in 1973 was criticized even more. (The latter refused to accept the prize.) There was no unanimous agreement in world public opinion, in 1976, when the prize was given to Amnesty International or in the following year when it went to the prime minister of Egypt, Anwar el-Sādāt, and the prime minister of Israel, Menachem Begin.

No one denied that these public figures had indeed worked on behalf of peace. Rather, the allegations focused on the principle of peace itself: working on behalf of peace was supposed to be the primary goal of these professional politicians in the first place. Should prizes be given to those who collect astronomical salaries and enjoy elevated status for doing their jobs?

If an area of disagreement concerning such designations had become almost generalized, it definitely existed in Norwegian society. The Norwegian Academy acted as the committee with the authority to grant the Nobel Prize for Peace (the other Nobel prizes are awarded from Sweden), and the uproar was the loudest in Norway.

As a result, a "parallel" Nobel prize was created: the Popular Prize for Peace. This award was to be decided by public vote, the recipient was to be truly worthy of the prize, and the award would include a large monetary gift. In 1973 the Popular Prize for Peace had greater resonance than ever when it went to Dom Helder Cámara, who had been repeatedly set aside by the Norwegian Academy and who, against predictions, was preferred over the Henry Kissinger–Le Duc Tho duo.

Giving the Nobel Prize for Peace to Mother Teresa led to the reconciliation of these two committees, official and popular, because the popular vote ratified the decision made by the academy.

The monetary award of the Nobel prize does not involve a fixed amount but varies according to the interest produced each year by the capital invested for the Alfred Nobel Foundation. The interest on the investments in 1979 allowed the total of the Nobel prize to reach $190,000. A note edited by the coordinator of the Norwegian Co-Workers for the work of Mother Teresa, Eli Werner, estimates the amount collected in the drive for the Popular Prize for Peace about equaled the Nobel.

As the recipient of both the official Nobel Prize for Peace and the Popular Prize for Peace, Mother Teresa returned to Calcutta with a check for approximately $400,000. The poor cared for by the Missionaries of Charity became its beneficiaries.

⌒

Even in the act of accepting the Nobel prize itself, Mother Teresa kept the poor closest to her heart. The celebration surrounding the award usually includes a gala dinner for hundreds of

dignitaries from around the world, including previous Nobel
winners. Mother Teresa, who had come to the Norwegian capital as the self-proclaimed representative of the poor, proposed
that, in place of the customary banquet, its equivalent cost be
destined for the poor. Naturally, the committee had no choice
but to accede to her reasonable request. Thus, the poor enjoyed a good supplement to their usual diet.

How many people would have been seated at the table had
the banquet for the Nobel prize taken place? Two, three, four
hundred? By an approximate calculation, fifteen thousand
people enjoyed that special banquet. Mother Teresa noted that
"for the poor, God does miracles every day."

∽

The same Providence that sustains "the birds of heaven and
the flowers of the field" (Matthew 6:26–30) guarantees daily
food to the thousands of poor that the Missionaries of Charity serve. Among those poor are the sisters themselves. They
ask nothing in return as they work long hours in a constant
service of love. Embracing the gospel challenge, they live as
the poorest among the poor.

To set up comparisons would be most inappropriate, even
unjust. But the social reality at the end of this century suggests
a reference that cannot be forgotten. Each religious congregation, male or female, has its own charism and its own specific
way of manifesting that charism but within a social context
that differs substantially from the social context in which the
majority of the congregations were founded.

All religious congregations have tried to adapt in response
to the discussions and documents of the Second Vatican Coun-

cil. In doing so, each hopes to conserve the spirit of its founder, given the fact that it would be impossible for the surrounding society to adapt to the founder's selfless spirit. This has meant that religious men and women, who in former times volunteered as social workers or teachers, now work as salaried social workers or teachers—with the same selfless spirit. (This is more prevalent in some countries than in others where, for example, healthcare, geriatrics, psychiatry, pediatrics, education, and other basic services have been socialized.) These people often hold their salaried positions more by force of circumstances than by preference.

This will never be true for the Missionaries of Charity, however, by reason of the very essence of their constitution. Mother Teresa left specific legislation rejecting any kind of fixed cash income for the work of the Missionaries of Charity. She did not accept working with the state or with other "political" institutions; today, her daughters carry on that same principle. Although the sisters frequently receive offers of government assistance, they graciously refuse; to accept would give them, presumably, a measure of security at odds with their professed total dependence on divine Providence.

On one occasion, Mother Teresa refused to accept an invitation that she felt was not compatible with the charism of the Missionaries of Charity:

> A bishop from Belgium had written us asking us to take charge of a very well-situated residence, and guaranteeing us a daily salary of some 250 rupees for each Sister. An attractive offer! I answered him: 'Bishop, I thank you very much for your offer, but we only accept the charge of people with handicaps,

impediments, and so forth. I am sorry, but it is not possible for us to do something contrary to this."

⌒

Mother Teresa did not embrace the popular notion that the quantity of a donation determines its worth. Rather, she asserted that the love with which the giving is offered determines its worth: "How much you give is not important; it's how much love you put into the giving."

Mother Teresa never fell into the egoism trap, even for the benefit of the poor. In one case, she praised publicly the generosity of Imperial Chemical Industries (ICI), a multinational corporation, for donating a building and land in Calcutta. She converted these resources into a model asylum—Prem Daan (Gift of Love)—for children with profound deficiencies. She also used the donations of another big company, the Hindustan Lever Company, to establish Asha Daan (Gift of Hope), an asylum for abandoned children.

Although she expressed gracious words of appreciation for these gifts, Mother Teresa displayed profound gratitude for the gift of a beggar who wanted to give her the little he had collected in one day. She had just received some important gifts at a gathering in her honor after she had won the Nobel prize, when the beggar approached her and said, "Mother Teresa, I see that everyone gives you gifts. I also want to give you something. Please do me the favor of accepting this. It is what I collected today."

It was little, but it was everything. Mother Teresa confessed that she was moved far deeper by the beggar's simple gesture than by the Nobel Prize for Peace. We can't help but recall that

Jesus, too, was moved more by the mite of the widow who, in her poverty, gave what she had to live on than with the offering of others who gave to God what was extra (Luke 21:3). "Don't give what's left over," Mother Teresa asked time and time again. "Give what costs you. Give till it hurts."

Mother Teresa discouraged people from going in search of the far-off poor of the Third World while overlooking the needy in one's own country, region, city, neighborhood, apartment, and family. She also discouraged people from focusing on purely material needs—which do exist—while neglecting to consider needs such as loneliness and sorrow, needs that are often more intense but less visible.

⁓

Few persons in the course of history have had as many friends as Mother Teresa. Among her friends were Malcolm Muggeridge, her first biographer, and Navin Chawla, another of her biographers; the Jesuits, Celeste Van Exem, Julien Henry, Edward Le Joly, and Ferdinand Perier; Monsignor Eric Barber; Michael Gomes; Ian Travers-Ball (Brother Andrew); Ann Blaikie; Eileen Egan; Violet and Frank Collins; Mother Anna Dengel; and Jacqueline de Decker, her "spiritual godmother," whom she came to know in Holy Family Hospital in Patna in 1948.

Other famous friends of Mother Teresa included the Australian James R. Knox, Vatican delegate in India and other countries, later archbishop of Melbourne and cardinal of the Roman Curia; Indira Gandhi; Queen Sophia of Spain; King Baudouin and Queen Fabiola of Belgium; Prince Philip, Duke of Edinburgh; Prince Charles and Princess Diana of Wales.

With their high public profiles, these friends to Mother Teresa are both known and easy to remember. But there were many others—religious and lay, rich and poor—who also forged real friendships with Mother Teresa. Many of them recall her warm and personal pleasure at greeting them, sometimes decades after the meeting, as if, at that moment, each was her only friend. Mother Teresa remembered events about their lives and asked about specific situations.

Once in 1980, far from India and Ireland, Mother Teresa met with a sister of Scottish origin, a sister of Our Lady of Loreto—the same institute to which Mother Teresa had belonged. The Scottish sister and Mother Teresa had gone through the novitiate in Darjeeling fifty years before.

The meeting was an emotional moment for both women. The happiest of the two outwardly seemed to be Mother Teresa, whereas the Scottish sister seemed to be rather shy. In spite of being surrounded by curious people and looking ahead to a busy schedule, Mother Teresa took the time to speak warmly to her old companion and to ask for news about their common friends. In the moment, she even welcomed the presence of the always intruding photographers. Taking her friend's hand, she willingly posed for pictures so that she could have a souvenir of the reunion.

⁓

On November 1, 1986, novices of the Missionaries of Charity professed their vows in San Gregorio al Celio in Rome. Mother Teresa was present for the celebration. Later that afternoon, in the company of four of the young women who had just professed their vows, Mother Teresa boarded a plane at Fiumcino destined for Madrid; the following day, she boarded a flight to Havana, Cuba. The small group was going to establish the congregation's first house on the Caribbean island.

On a previous visit to Cuba, to "get to know the territory," Mother Teresa had met with Fidel Castro. She later recalled to the author that at one point in the conversation, which had been more like a monologue on Castro's part ("He talked and talked," as Mother Teresa described it with gentle irony), the opportunity for true dialogue presented itself:

Castro: Let's see, Mother, what is the work which your Sisters propose to do in Cuba?

Mother Teresa: The Sisters are coming to work for the poorest of the poor.

Castro: Well, here, after the Revolution, the class of poor people no longer exists. Here, thanks to the Revolution, everyone has work and all Cubans have their basic necessities taken care of. Our healthcare and educational systems figure among the best in the world.

Mother Teresa: Very fine, Mister President. But are there not people here who find themselves alone, children abandoned by their parents, single mothers and their children abandoned, old people neglected by their families, alcoholics, here where they have so much rum? Are there not former prisoners here who have no place to go when they get out of jail?

Castro: Are you telling me, Mother, that you and your sisters bother with that type of person?

Mother Teresa: Yes, Mister President. Those persons also are children of God. Yes, we work for them.

Castro: Ah, well, then. Come, Mother. The Revolution and the Cuban people welcome you.

⌒

Ready generosity is required in the act of giving. There are those who, without knowing it, have a great deal but give very little—if at all. They don't know how to give. Then there are those who have little but give a lot. Mother Teresa's life was the perfect embodiment—almost beyond words—of the verb *to give.*

Above all, Mother Teresa taught by her own example. She taught people to give of themselves. When she explained the degrees of giving, she certainly did not exclude giving *things* or *money.* But she was always quick to admonish us to share that which we have beyond our material wealth: compassion, time, and love. Even more, she challenged us to give of ourselves until it hurt, until it "cost" us.

Mother Teresa often told the story of an Australian gentleman who wanted to give a donation. "Right away he said, 'This is something which does not affect me directly. I want to give something of myself.' From then on, he came regularly to our Home for the Dying to shave the sick men and to talk with them. Not only was he generous with his money but with his time. He could have used both things—his money and his time—for himself. He was generous with himself."

If we do not know much about the generosity of individuals toward the work of the Missionaries of Charity, it is only because Mother Teresa preferred discretion. The reason was not that she liked secrecy—she kept the accounts and taught others to keep them to the penny out of respect for the donors. Rather, Mother Teresa wanted every donation, regardless of amount, credited to a determined purpose and then used for that purpose and no other. "Don't even think that a gesture, as small as it may be, in favor of your neighbors, lacks value. What pleases God is not how much we do, but with how much love we do it. In this, God is seen, because God is love. He has made us in his image: to love and be loved."

~

In communion with the Missionaries of Charity and their spirit of family, there are Co-Workers around the world who constitute dynamic and specific groups. There are healthcare Co-Workers, priest Co-Workers, sick Co-Workers, and Co-Workers with vows who are more properly called Lay Missionaries of Charity.

Without becoming a separate group, even the staffs of various airline companies enjoyed opportunities for "collaboration" with Mother Teresa over the years. A few of them—Air India, Alitalia, Pan American (now defunct), British Airways, Air France, TWA, Swissair, and Iberia—often had the privilege of Mother Teresa traveling on board their planes. Following Air India's initiative, various airline companies offered Mother Teresa free airfare. As a passenger, Mother Teresa was often asked to give her autograph and to engage in serious conversation.

Some of those conversations had dramatic consequences. For example, some female flight attendants, after listening to Mother Teresa's comments, exchanged their flight uniforms for the blue-and-white saris of the Missionaries of Charity. They chose to attend to the needs of the poorest of the poor in the slums instead of the needs of airline passengers. Rather than performing their duties routinely and for pay, they performed them with and for love.

In other instances, flight attendants used their layover time to help the sisters in local soup kitchens for the poor in the slums. One attendant accepted the responsibility of accompanying children given for adoption to parents in far-off countries.

⌒

Eileen Egan narrated the following incident to Brother Luke, provincial superior of the brothers in the United States. Brother Luke, in turn, wrote about the incident in the 1992 issue of the Christmas newsletter that he traditionally sends to brothers and Co-Workers.

> One time, in my presence, the religion editor of an international magazine was doing an interview with Mother Teresa. To one of the questions, Mother Teresa answered that she was acutely convinced of the sacredness of life, including that of the unborn. The interviewer wanted to know if killing was ever justified, for example, in the case of war. Mother Teresa shook her head no. She didn't say a word, but gave clear indications that she was not in agreement, in any case, with the suppression of life. The journalist insisted: "Look, Mother, the Church teaches that war can be justified." Mother Teresa continued to shake her head and repeat: "I cannot believe it." The reporter didn't give up: "Catholics

have to accept that doctrine of the Church." Mother Teresa looked at him and, with unaccustomed vehemence, returned the question to him: "Then, am I not a Catholic?"

~

Brother Andrew said: "Whatever may be the image one has of Mother Teresa, it has to be admitted that she possesses a slightly mischievous sense of humor. My own experience is that she is not able to hold back a happy smile at the joke about how she kidnapped me from the Jesuits."

As a cofounder with Mother Teresa of the Missionary Brothers of Charity, Brother Andrew was privileged to have a close relationship with Mother Teresa. As a result, he has never made a myth of her or her work.

When Brother Andrew first met with the candidates for the brothers, he found them to be a group of young, uncultivated men who were guided by the sisters. "Actually," he noted "too guided by them, to the point that I would dare say, at the risk of being called a chauvinist, that I had to do my darndest to liberate them."

Brother Andrew was a good Jesuit before he became a Missionary Brother of Charity. As a result, he tried to inculcate in the young candidates an Ignatian spirit. "Mother Teresa," he said, "did not welcome the changes I was introducing, but I have to confess that she respected the responsibility she had given me. She could disagree with me in small details, but she never lost confidence in me. And that made me feel peaceful."

He added: "We were different, obviously. I annoyed her in little ways. Sometimes I felt contradicted by some of her actions, sometimes she felt the same toward me. But she is a woman whose love and interest in others is much more profound than her disagreement with their ideas or talents."

Brother Andrew remained the head of the brothers for twenty years, years that spiritually formed the congregation. Besides being cofounder, Brother Andrew was inspirer and "servant."

By 1988 Brother Andrew believed that the congregation had reached a mature level and he stepped down. He returned to Australia to preach the exercises of Ignatius and to raise awareness about the plight of the poor in a spirit between that of Mother Teresa and Ignatius.

In the fall of 1991, Brother Andrew made one of his many trips to Calcutta and visited with Mother Teresa. He painted a beautiful picture of the meeting:

> I found her aged. She had been ill. She appears fragile. Her voice is weaker. But to hear her speak of some of the tasks on which she is embarked leaves the impression of a woman very much of today, of an extraordinary personality. An hour is sufficient to hear her say that she has opened seven communities of Sisters in Russia and that others are on the way; that fifteen young Albanian women have entered her Congregation, some of whom have had to be baptized due to the severe repression over the years. And that she has postulants also in Romania and Hungary.
>
> She has established seven communities in Cuba in the last two or three years, and she is in contact with Fidel Castro. One sees a mutual esteem be-

tween the two, without downplaying the fact that
each one preserves his or her very diverse beliefs.
She told us about a United States governor who tele-
phoned her to ask what decision he should make
about a convicted man on death row. She told him,
"Do what Jesus would have done." A week later the
news got around that the governor commuted the
man's sentence to life in prison.

The law in Albania considered religious worship
punishable with the death penalty. The president
asked Mother Teresa to open six churches that had
been used for profane purposes. She underlines with
roguishness: "I also opened a mosque for the Moslems." Before that, she helped her Sisters mop it.
Needless to say, the relations between Christians and
Moslems could not have gotten a better start in Albania.

⁓

On important feasts such as Christmas, the Missionaries of
Charity and their Co-Workers routinely visit prisons. They
take each inmate a simple, significant, practical gift (an article
of clothing, stockings for women, socks for men, and so forth)
and something to eat.

On one occasion, before going to a women's jail of four hundred inmates, the Missionaries of Charity asked the owner of
a medium-sized textile company to provide them with hundreds of pairs of socks. For some reason, the manufacturer
took note of his client's address, which appeared to be that of
a typical little convent, and decided to make the delivery him-

A Legacy of Love

self. Upon arrival, he found himself at a soup kitchen where, every day except Thursdays, the poor were fed and given medicines. On that particular day, several hundred people were waiting to be fed.

The man asked for the superior. Already surprised by what he observed, he was further surprised when he was introduced to a sister of foreign face and tongue, with humble and loving attitude and ways, who was wearing an apron.

The factory owner asked Mother Teresa where she wanted him to put the merchandise. When Mother Teresa moved as if to lift some boxes, the man stopped her. He insisted on unloading the truck himself—and then tore up the bill.

∽

"The poor are wonderful people" is an expression frequently on the lips of Mother Teresa. Because she has devoted her life as a voice to the world for the poor, because of the unlimited goodness of her heart toward the poor, and because she has worked in direct contact with the poor, Mother Teresa knows what she is talking about: the poor are a concrete, daily, continual reality for her and always with her. She is an expert on the poor. Watching them with eyes full of kindness and understanding, she is totally devoid of prejudice or judgment.

Considering Mother Teresa's love and compassion for the poor, we can understand why she considered them "wonderful people." The story of the heroism of a poor woman burdened with small children can serve to illustrate the poor's "wonderful" quality.

One day, Mother Teresa heard about a woman and her children who had gone several days without anything to eat.

Mother Teresa quickly gathered a generous ration of rice and took it to the woman and her children.

As soon as Mother Teresa arrived with the rice, the children's mother left with half the ration but returned shortly. A surprised Mother Teresa asked the woman where she had gone and what she had done. "Our next-door neighbor, together with her children, have gone the same number of days as we have without eating. I wanted to share with them what you brought to us."

On many occasions—and with great emotion—Mother Teresa recalled this story. At times she added a significant detail to emphasize her central message that "the poor are wonderful people": one family was Buddhist, the other was Moslem.

Countless other episodes exemplify Mother Teresa's wisdom about the "wonderful" goodness of the poor:

- the starving girl who refused to eat the bread the sisters offered her; she wanted to take it to her sick father
- the boy who fled the warmth and shelter the sisters offered to be with his mother, whose home consisted of no more than an old mat under the branches of a tree
- the Mexican-American man who was so poor that he kept the cadaver of his wife in his house for several days because, despite his begging, he couldn't manage to collect enough money to pay for a coffin
- the Australian aborigine who would not disclose the name of the man who brutally beat him: "If they punish him, that won't heal the wounds."

If Mother Teresa's first visit to the former Soviet Union (the Commonwealth of Independent States) had happened after 1991, the trip would have been less newsworthy. But she went in August 1987, when the political landscape looked considerably different. Although the visit was worthy of front-page coverage, it received no headline; the visit was kept low key. Mother Teresa avoided as much publicity as she possibly could.

Traveling almost incognito from London's Heathrow Airport to Moscow, Mother Teresa visited the Soviet Union at the invitation of the Soviet Committee for Peace. The invitation was the result of a film that two Canadian sisters, Ann and Jeannette Petrie, had made about Mother Teresa and her work. *The World of Mother Teresa* had premiered at the United Nations and had been aired on television in nearly every country of the world. It eventually reached the Film Festival of Moscow, where the Soviet Committee for Peace awarded it the prize of that same name, with a gold medal for the "star" of the film.

Something special for Mother Teresa? No. As usual, she kept a low profile and traveled light: a two-handled cloth bag for her austere necessities and a couple of cardboard boxes tied with string. In the boxes, she carried a statue of the Virgin, some medals, holy cards of the Miraculous Virgin, and rosaries. The only reporter who managed to find out about the trip appeared at the airport with the illusion of getting an exclusive story. Instead, he managed to pull out of Mother Teresa only a few words: "I would like to take Jesus wherever I go."

The visit generated a moderate amount of news coverage, at least in Moscow. One news story included a photograph of Mother Teresa giving a news conference in the shadow of a large portrait of Karl Marx. A few news agencies carried a photograph of Mother Teresa accepting a bouquet of flowers and the gold medal from Genrikh Borovik, then president of the Soviet Committee for Peace. The media also gave an account of the brief conversation between the two. Mother Teresa invited the Soviet people "to give God thanks for everything." Borovik responded: "What you call God, we call Nature. I think that we are referring to the same thing." Only after Mother Teresa left Moscow did it become known that the Soviet authorities acceded to her desire to visit a center for the survivors of the nuclear catastrophe in Chernobyl, which had occurred in April 1986.

Back home, Mother Teresa was a little more disposed to talk about her Moscow visit. "They could not have been more kind to me," she said. "They spoke about God with all naturalness. I don't think they wanted to take advantage of my presence. I had the impression that the desire for peace on the part of everyone is sincere."

Scarcely was news out about the visit before a great amount of curiosity arose: Did Mother Teresa meet with President Mikhail Gorbachev? Was Mother Teresa going to open a house in the Soviet Union? Mother Teresa herself addressed the issues: she had not met with Mikhail Gorbachev, who was absent from Moscow at the time. She had, however, written him a letter. About opening a house, she explained with prudent realism that, in the Soviet Union, the Orthodox Church did not have permission to promote works of charity because the government reserved any charitable task solely for itself. She pointed out that before a charitable foundation could be established in the Soviet Union, existing laws would have to be changed. Borovik himself had said that it was too soon to suggest the topic of a foundation of the Missionaries of Charity in Russia; besides the fact that it would have been an event without precedent, it would have been precipitous for the *glasnost* process then taking its course. The idea needed time to be assimilated.

Mother Teresa displayed no impatience with the situation. She once again affirmed that, after doing everything possible, she would wait on God. If things did not work out, she said, she would see that as a sign of God's will. As usual, the sign that she eventually received, as was most often the case, confirmed that her will, indeed, coincided with God's.

Mother Teresa's first trip to Moscow was the sowing of a seed. She had forged an emotional link between herself and the Russians—both the ruling class and the common people. This link would bring her goodness back to their country to serve the needy in the near future.

In December 1988 a severe earthquake shook Armenia. Tens of thousands of children, women, and old people needed to be evacuated. One of the first to offer assistance was Mother Teresa: "I bring neither gold nor silver, but I hope to be able to offer the help of my volunteers for the rebuilding process." Without fanfare, the Moscow press released the following news item: "The Missionaries of Charity of Mother Teresa have received permission to work in the Soviet Union on behalf of the elderly, the homeless, and the handicapped. It is the first time since the Russian Revolution that a foreign institution has been given authorization to operate in the U.S.S.R."

Shortly after they obtained permission to enter the Soviet Union, the Missionaries of Charity established two foundations. The municipal authorities of Moscow put two buildings at their disposal, one in the district of Pervomaski and another in the district of Vorochilovski. The sisters arrived ready to carry out the most difficult tasks but were open to accepting the help of anyone willing to volunteer. It didn't matter to them if the volunteers were believers or atheists.

Although the donated buildings were in need of restoration, Providence saw to it, as usual, that the sisters had what they needed. An Italian company with business dealings in Leningrad offered to restore, free of charge, one of the buildings; a Dutch company offered to restore the other.

Today, the homes of the Missionaries of Charity in the former Soviet Union operate much like their homes in other parts of the world. The number of sisters dedicated to a particular task is similar to the number engaged in the same task in other countries. Adaptations are made to cope with the extreme economic hardship that has followed the transition from a state-run economy to a market economy, which has led to the rise of opportunistic speculators and the extreme poverty of the masses. The sisters also have had to adapt to the social consequences of widespread addiction to vodka, which continues to be sold at a price incredibly low in a country where everything else has become expensive.

All this began with the awarding of a prize.

In 1990 the Soviet government awarded a more significant prize to Mother Teresa: the International Leo Tolstoy Medal, described as "the most important award which the Soviet Foundation for Children gives to a person who, by way of his or her labor, courage, and actions, distinguishes himself or herself in assistance to the children of the whole world." According to its announcement, the committee of the foundation selected Mother Teresa "for the example which she gives of love for the poor and, in a special way, for children and orphans," now that she "is a living symbol of humanity, generosity, and love which teaches us all how we ought to love others."

⤴

Mother Teresa's relationship with Albania, of course, had a particular significance: Albania was her place of birth, from which, for many reasons, she had been obliged to remain distant for nearly sixty years. Although impassable frontiers opened for her, she had been shut out of her own homeland.

It's easy to understand why Mother Teresa's first visit to her native country would be joyful; however, she was not particularly vocal about it. While there, she took the opportunity to kneel before the tomb that holds the remains of her sister, Aga, and her mother, Drana. Before visiting the tomb, Mother Teresa stopped at Skopje, where she saw the destruction caused by the 1963 earthquake. The house where she was born had totally disappeared, as had the parish Church of the Sacred Heart of Jesus.

Later, in a 1990 Christmas letter to her Co-Workers, Mother Teresa commented on the work being done in her homeland:

> Glory and honor to God for all that he has done for us in Albania, whose inhabitants have such hunger for him. Our Sisters are doing a beautiful work in three homes there (two in Tirana and one in Schodra), opening minds and hearts to Jesus in a splendid way. In Tirana we have a home for the abandoned sick; in Schodra we have a home for children with physical and psychological disabilities. We have opened the Cathedral of Tirana, which

had been converted into a movie house. Imagine the joy of the Sacred Heart when we opened the cathedral with a Mass in which thousands of people participated!

~

Mother Teresa entered into the very heart of the Gulf War. In a letter of June 23, 1991, sent from Baghdad, epicenter of the war, to her Co-Workers throughout the world, Mother Teresa said:

It is an authentic miracle of the tenderness of God that the government of Iraq has permitted us to come to found a center of Missionaries of Charity in the very center of Baghdad, in a locale which the government itself gave us. A great number of important people have collaborated with us in re-conditioning the location, which soon will be filled to overflowing with malnourished and mutilated children. The government has offered us a van to be used as a mobile clinic, since the poor live far away and are incapable of covering long distances. They have asked us to open two more homes.

How tremendous are the consequences of the war! It seems impossible to understand how human beings can do such things to one another. Why? One notices an enormous scarcity of food and medicines. Since hundreds and hundreds of homes have been destroyed, I do not have the slightest idea of the time that it will take to reconstruct it all. Let us include Iraq in the intentions of our daily prayers.

Never would I have dared think that our presence would produce such joy for thousands of persons who suffer so much everywhere. Among our Sisters, there are some who speak Arabic, so that will make things somewhat easier. Observing the terrible sufferings and the consequences of war, it occurs to me that what we destroyed are not only buildings, but the very core of love, of peace, and of union.

~

One of the most unforgettable stories Mother Teresa told was about a woman who, like many people in Calcutta, had been born and raised in the streets without ever knowing the protection and warmth of a home. Mother Teresa found this woman dying in the street. Her body was covered with worms and a gangrenous leg had been half-gnawed by rats. Mother Teresa picked her up, carried her to Nirmal Hriday, bathed her in warm water, and placed her in a bed.

The dying woman struggled to express what she was feeling. Finally, she managed a few final words: "I have lived like an animal in the streets. This is the first time that my body has rested between two sheets. Finally, I am going to die like a human being, surrounded by love and by care."

Mother Teresa often told this story and ended it with: "A most beautiful smile formed on her lips. Perhaps never in my life have I seen a smile as serene as that."

~

When local elections were held in Bengala, Mother Teresa considered it her duty to vote. One of the candidates, who had no more reason to believe that Mother Teresa's vote would be against his party as to think it would be for it, brought to her attention a slight nuance: "Mother Teresa, you ought not vote. You do not belong to any party. You belong equally to all of us."

As a result, Mother Teresa abstained from voting—and she never voted in her life. She took to heart what the candidate had said. She truly was with all people and for all people; she would not risk appearances to the contrary.

Mother Teresa's decision not to participate in elections, of course, did not mean she lacked convictions; she had many, even in the realm of politics. Her convictions, however, always placed the rights of the least protected first and foremost. Always lovable, with an amiability that increased as she grew older, she allowed a holy ire to flower whenever she noticed that someone intended to profit from the poor.

This holy ire came to the surface, for example, in a Latin American country where she was determined to acquire a piece of property next to the parish where her sisters were working. She began the appropriate procedures armed with her convictions: that in the poor, she was seeking lodging for Jesus. Her genuine amiability appeared to find an echo in the seller's way of speaking. He laid it on thick when he tried to camouflage the price and make the deal look like he was offering Mother Teresa preferential consideration on behalf of the poor.

As soon as she heard the asking price quoted in local money, however, Mother Teresa did a quick mental conversion into dollars. "No, thank you," she responded. "Don't play around with the poor!" And she tore up the contract.

The witness of the scene, a Co-Worker who felt himself privileged to have driven Mother Teresa to the property, heard her comment during the return drive: "Good heavens! I don't know what would have happened if I had accepted his offer. The price he asked for his property is triple what's paid in the area."

The driver admitted that he didn't know what to admire more: Mother Teresa's courage in the face of immoral business tactics or her pragmatism in being abreast of the prices of real estate in a country far from her mother India.

⁓

Between 1984 and 1985, news items began to appear and were being discussed in the streets about one of the most cruel evils to appear near the end of the twentieth century—acquired immune deficiency syndrome (AIDS). Medical science, in full battle against cancer, was boasting of the increased survival odds for cancer patients when the new plague appeared. Although titanic efforts ensued to develop a vaccine, most AIDS victims died more or less unnoticed unless they were Hollywood stars or renowned authors.

Great ostracism developed against the carriers of the mysterious virus. A person with AIDS was human scum to be avoided for two reasons: the danger of contracting the fatal illness and the stigma attached to the illness itself.

Mother Teresa, along with others, saw the needs of the poor in the midst of the situation. As usual, she found the identity of Jesus applicable to the victims of AIDS. She saw Jesus in those who suffered both the pain of the disease and the resulting lack of affection from their brothers and sisters.

Beginning with the terminally ill, Mother Teresa embarked

on her project where the ostracism was the worst—New York City. She asked the mayor for a local site and assured him that she and her sisters would take charge of the most desperate patients and help them to die in the company of God.

Because some of the residents near the proposed site were against the idea, the mayor initially didn't have the courage to grant Mother Teresa her request. Eventually, however, he changed his mind and told the opposing residents, "Would you know how to deny something requested by a living saint? Mother Teresa is perhaps the only living saint there is today. It was she who asked me for it personally. I can't deny it to her."

The mayor gave Mother Teresa a structure that had room for fifteen beds. Her first boarders were three prisoners on the verge of dying. Out of fear of infection, not even their prison mates wanted to be near them. The first to die was a Vietnam veteran who, after returning traumatized from the war, had succumbed to drugs and contracted AIDS through a blood transfusion. More than the others, he was grateful for the care and shelter provided by Mother Teresa and her sisters. He felt attracted to religion, asked to be baptized, and died peacefully. In his last moments, he confessed, "Without this infirmity, I do not believe that I would have ever returned to God. For that reason, I accept it from his hands, and I thank him."

The heroic courage of Mother Teresa and her sisters enlivened consciences and awoke admiration. President Ronald Reagan asked Mother Teresa to open an AIDS home in Washington, D.C., and provided a locale. The home was inaugurated "Gift of Peace" in November 1986.

Peace is, paradoxically, what people who are terminally ill with AIDS tend to find in the shelters provided for their care. Mother Teresa told the story of one:

One of our residents, infected with AIDS in its last stages, had to be admitted to the hospital. He found out that I had come on a visit and called for me. He said he wanted to have a conversation alone with me. He confided to me that when his headache was the strongest, he remembered Jesus crowned with thorns. When his pain most affected his back, he thought of the lashes that Jesus suffered while he was tied to the pillar. That if his hands or feet gave him the most pain, he thought of the nails in Jesus' body. He begged that he be allowed to die near us. We obtained permission from the doctor to bring him back to the home. No sooner had he arrived, than he wanted to go to the chapel. I observed him pray with great devotion. After three days, he died. His was an admirable death and very serene.

Chapter 7

THE SPIRIT OF
MOTHER TERESA IN OTHERS

Mother Teresa inspired generosity and goodness in every corner of the world. Besides the countless parables about the power of her own personal example, stories of the influence of her spirit will continue to motivate and challenge. Although the following accounts have been gleaned from resent history, they—and many more yet to be known will fashion a legacy of goodness that the world will never forget.

～

The spirit of Mother Teresa's work is characterized by the idea that charitable assistance must be provided without the desire for publicity. ("Let your left hand…" Matthew 6:3.) The sisters abhor the idea of anyone attempting to take advantage of the poor. Sometimes, however, this is precisely what happens.

Such was the case of a Latin American banana grower who

wanted to provide all the bananas that the "good sisters" needed for their "poor little ones." The "good sisters" declined the gift when they learned that the banana grower planned to use his charitable gesture as a publicity stunt by trumpeting the fact that he provided bananas to the poor of Mother Teresa of Calcutta.

Consider, on the other hand, the example of an important man who owned several businesses, among them a hotel chain. He was a good Catholic and an admirer and benefactor of Mother Teresa and her sisters.

One Christmas day the businessman offered to provide a dinner for all the poor in the slum where the Missionaries of Charity had their soup kitchen. He offered to host the dinner at his downtown hotel, the best one in his chain. That day, the hotel would be closed to its regular clientele and reserved for the poor.

The sisters accepted the man's offer, and a total of 250 needy people showed up. The hotel staff, dressed in their gala uniforms, served them as though they were VIPs. Even the mayor of the city honored the poor by serving the first plate of spaghetti. That night, the radio and television newscasts highlighted the event, and it was big news in the major newspapers the next morning.

Everything seemed fine to everyone except the sisters, but they didn't say a word. The following year, when the hotel owner enthusiastically offered to repeat the gesture, the sisters hesitated. They thanked him for his generosity but let him know that they hadn't liked the tone of the publicity that his noble gesture had stirred up the previous year. Unlike the banana grower, however, this particular businessman was not interested in the publicity but in the spirit of giving.

That Christmas the businessman brought his entire family with him to the sports complex where the special meal for the poor was served. He personally took part in serving the food and did the same thing in following years.

∽

In May 1990, a small community of the Missionaries of Charity was established in Glasgow, Scotland. Within a short time, some of the neighbors complained. The four sisters were making too much noise with their singing at five o'clock in the morning. What's more, many of the people who showed up every day to pray with the sisters rang neighbors' doorbells by mistake.

Other neighbors, however, said that all the world admired the sisters' work and if the sisters had to leave their current home, the city council should offer them an adequate residence free of charge.

The township put the subject to a vote, and the sisters won the right to remain where they were.

∽

Many people believe that the global reality Mother Teresa called Providence acts by secondary causes. In other words, God usually makes use of people.

For example, instead of miraculously filling the sisters' pantry, clothing racks, or medicine chest during the night, God softly awakens a giving heart in people of generous means, often when these people have more than enough.

When least expected, a truck driver arrives at a soup kitchen and says, "Let's see, Mother. I've been given this, paid in full, to be delivered at this address. Where do you want me to put it?"

It usually happens that the truck driver, not knowing much about the sisters in the strange dresses and assuming that it's all for a good purpose, pleads, "No, please, Mother. Tell me where, and I'll unload the truck myself."

Once the task is finished, the truck driver, shyly and respectfully, often asks the sister to do him the favor of signing the invoice, of which he leaves a copy. The truck driver hesitates as he shakes sister's hand and—something that he would not do in other cases—stubbornly refuses a tip. "For the Lord's sake, Mother, no, not in this case. You people are special."

Although the sister has an invoice, she has no intention of keeping a detailed file of benefactors to be approached later for further assistance. Rather, she keeps the invoice so she can send a few words of gratitude in the name of the poor. The Missionaries of Charity leave the business of a computerized list in the hands of Providence. The information they keep is minimal. They will use it later when they ask God to reward those who love him and help the poor.

~

One Saturday morning, a Co-Worker rang the doorbell of the Missionaries of Charity's home located on the city's outskirts. No one answered, an evident sign that all the members of the little community were away in their ministries of charity. The visitor decided to wait for the sisters to return.

As the Co-Worker waited for the sisters, he saw an elderly man timidly approach the sisters' home. The man appeared to be from the countryside and walked wearily with the support of a cane. The following conversation ensued:

Elderly man: Is this where some sisters called Missionaries of Charity live, the ones who have something to do with Mother Teresa, the one who received an important prize some years ago?

Co-Worker: Yes. If I'm not mistaken, this is the first time you've ever been here. Am I right?

Elderly man: Yes. It's the first time I've ever come to this area in more than seventy years of walking in this city. It has cost me a great deal to come—from the bus station. If I hadn't taken a taxi, I don't know how I would have made it here. Even the cab driver seemed a bit nervous about coming here; after all, that good man didn't have any idea who these sisters are. "I don't know anything about priests and nuns. To me they're all the same," the cab driver told me.

Co-Worker: Good. You know that it is almost never easy the first time you try to get to a place you're not familiar with. At any rate, next time you come to see the Missionaries of Charity, you'll see how easy it will be.

Elderly man: I've come to fulfill the wishes of my deceased wife, but after this, I'll have no reason to return. What's more, if you know the sisters well, which I think you do, you may give them what I've brought them, and then I can be on my way. I would like to be home before dark.

Co-Worker: I will do it gladly, but I don't believe they will be long. Wouldn't you be interested in getting to know them and give them in person what you have brought?

Elderly man: No. I think you are a person that can be trusted. What I am bringing them is valuable in the heart of my deceased wife; it doesn't become any more valuable if I give it personally. I understand that good works are better if they are done without attracting attention, which goes better with my way of doing things. If God sees it, that's enough.

Co-Worker: You honor me, my good man. I will do the favor you ask. But it must be obvious to you that I am humbled to be the intermediary for such a noble person.

Elderly man: No, please. There's nothing noble about me. I'm a simple country man. I've had all kinds of jobs. My wife and I didn't have any children, but we always got along very well. Three years ago, she came down with cancer. We buried her two weeks ago. Even though she never liked to show off, she kept some jewels—a couple of rings, earrings, some necklaces, gifts that I had given her at our wedding and on our anniversaries. Personally, I wish she had taken the wedding rings with her to the grave, but she had planned otherwise, and I respect that decision. A little before her death, she confided in me a long-held desire: that the jewels be given to the poor of Mother Teresa of Calcutta. She liked Mother Teresa very much, ever since she read a book about her that she always had at her bedside and which she continued to read while she could still see. I'm giving the jewels to you in the same simple box where she kept them.

Co-Worker: Well, if that is what you want, I will hand your gift over to the sisters. But I assure you, I don't know whether I feel more moved or humbled by this request. Since I know that the sisters like to reply with a thank-you note any time they receive something, I would appreciate it if you would give me your address so they may send you a little note.

Elderly man: No, please. I don't want that. My deceased wife would not have wanted that either. You can tell them to pray

for her and for me and then we'll be even. I've already told
you: I probably will not be coming back here again. I've
decided to make out my will to these sisters who strike me
as people who will make good use of the money from the
jewels.

Co-Worker: I'm sure they will. I will pray, too, though I think
that a person as good as your deceased wife must be in better circumstances to pray for us. In any case, prayers are
never lost, just as what we do for the poor is never lost.

Elderly man: Thank you so much, sir.

With solemn admiration, the Co-Worker watched the elderly
man, leaning on his cane, set off again on his journey.

⁓

It never rains much in Madrid. In fact, there are winters when
it rains very little. At times, however, it rains steadily for days.

One day when it began to rain, a group of neighbors saw an
old lady seated on a bench in a small square near the downtown area. Unbelievably, the woman was still there the following day in spite of the nonstop rain.

One of the observers commented to another: "My God! How
horrible! Not even in Somalia would we see something like
this! What can be done?"

The other answered: "I understand that in the area around
the Manzanares River there are some Indian nuns who dedicate themselves to finding abandoned people."

The neighbors inquired further and finally contacted the
Missionaries of Charity. In turn, the sisters called Mercedes
(Suarez Guanes), coordinator of the Co-Workers of Mother

Teresa in Spain (and eventually of all Co-Workers in southern Europe). With a surprising capacity for doing meritorious things without considering them very important, Mercedes drove to the square, picked up the shivering woman, and drove her to the shelter of the Immaculate Heart of Mary of the Missionaries of Charity. Mercedes bathed the woman, changed her clothing, and put her to bed. All the while, the woman did not utter a sound. Only when Mercedes was on her way out did she notice that the old woman gave her a slight smile. Perhaps it was the woman's first smile in a long time; perhaps it was her last. The following morning Mercedes called to inquire about the old lady. She was told that the woman had been found dead at six that morning, with a serene smile on her face.

∽

An anecdote narrated by Co-Worker Mario Bertini took place during the Christmas season. One Sunday afternoon, the superior of the house in Castello, Italy, a shelter for single mothers, decided that all mothers and their children would go to the circus. Bertini, whose generous volunteering included, among other things, acting as chauffeur, was in charge of taking the group.

Besides being the driver, Bertini attempted to be the sisters' financial advisor. When he first heard that the superior intended to take the mothers and their children to the circus that afternoon, he suggested they consider going on a weekday when the admission price would be lower. But the superior wanted to go on Sunday, the only day the mothers had free from work outside the home.

At the circus, Bertini tried to convince the ticket-taker to give the group the lowest possible prices available in general seating. When the ticket-taker suggested they come on a weekday, the superior again insisted that the mothers and their children couldn't come at any other time except Sunday afternoon.

While everybody emptied their pockets to pool their money together—still coming up short for the entire admission cost—a portion of the tent flap parted, and a well-dressed man appeared. "Sister," he said, "settle a question for me. Are you the Sisters of Mother Teresa of Calcutta?"

The superior responded, "Yes, and these are our mothers with their children."

"Well, fine," the man said with enthusiasm. "What are you waiting for? How many are there? Thirty? Let's go. There ought to be room in the preferred seating. But hurry, the show is about to begin."

When Bertini gets to this point, he flashes a smile and concludes, "Needless to say, we went to the show free of charge. And it was for all, especially for the smallest, an unforgettable afternoon."

⌐

The Co-Workers of Mother Teresa and the work they do for the poor in Anchorage, Alaska, have special characteristics. Bob Eaton, coordinator, gave an account of the Co-Workers' situation in that remote area.

It seems the homeless are in great distress, especially when the temperatures drop to thirty-five to fifty degrees below zero. Bob says:

> In such circumstances, the only objective is to survive. In order to not perish in the cold on the streets

during the night, the poor begin to come to the shelter around four in the afternoon, dragging along their few belongings in plastic bags. The old people and the sick are the first to look for a place to begin to warm themselves. Following that, the others arrive. At supper time, there are never less than three hundred persons at the shelter, which is just an old warehouse for storing snow removal equipment. Some volunteers, including some among the needy themselves, take charge to maintain and clean it. Others are totally incapable of taking care of themselves. The latter are, for the most part, the mentally ill and alcoholics. For them, the shelter represents their only refuge from the deadly cold, their only chance of getting a good warm meal.

∽

The Portuguese Co-Workers in Setubal, who provided lodging for the first house of the Missionaries of Charity in Portugal, tell the following story. In their home in Setubal for abandoned and disabled children, Jacinta was the most handicapped of all. She was so deformed that she had no eyes, ears, or fingers.

On Christmas, the Co-Workers welcome the children in their homes for a few days. The family that welcomed little Jacinta decided to look for specialized help for her. She was taken to France, where she was successfully operated on to restore her hearing. An operation to restore her sight will follow and then another to fit her little hands with fingers.

∽

In Faro, in southern Portugal, the Co-Workers like to tell the strange story of a man who was notorious for drinking and stealing. He was welcomed by the sisters into their home for needy persons in spite of protests by the neighbors, who knew of the man's reputation. Nevertheless, the man moved in. Four months later, he died in peace. Those who were witnesses of the two facts—the man's spiritual transformation and his peaceful death—believe that God called the man directly through the loving presence of the Missionaries of Charity.

⤶

Countless stories attest to the profound good that the Co-Workers and the Missionaries of Charity have brought to the lives of others. One of these stories comes from Great Britain.

> I have been limited for five years from doing anything but caring for a disabled grandson. Each day of his life has brought me closer to God, praying to him with love. My grandson challenges me in silence—because he is totally mute—to force myself to be an optimistic Christian. Also, he pushes me delicately—since he lacks the strength in his paralyzed hands—to carry out my tasks day after day.
>
> Through my grandson's atrophied cerebrum, the Lord has taught me the meaning of true love, which is not in receiving but in giving and in pardoning those who do us harm. In the opinion of some people, my grandson and those who are in conditions like his are a burden on society. I am convinced that the gift of my grandson for me consists in be-

ing able to love and serve him, since, as Mother Teresa assures, each time we do something for the poor, we do it for God. In my daily work and through my belonging to a worldwide organization such as that of the Co-Workers, I have come to discover that my love for God in my neighbor becomes concrete for me in identifying Christ in my grandson.

〜

A Co-Worker from South Africa shares this story.

I am a Co-Worker from when the association was born in Zimbabwe. I have two children, a boy and a girl, who are both teenagers. My husband is a pilot, so it falls to me to be mother, father, mechanic, plumber, electrician, and so forth. I carry out my work as a Co-Worker in a home for the elderly.

For several years I have been friend to a woman about fifty years old who is a total invalid. She can neither speak nor move, but fortunately, we understand each other perfectly and share moments of real happiness. Her name is Marlene and she is a marvelous person who helps me a great deal to stay humble. It has been a privilege for me to know her.

One day a week I help the woman in charge of the home, so she can do other things. Obviously, I try to remember that I owe my time to my husband and children before all else. Sometimes it bothers me that I am not doing enough, but then I recall the words of Mother Teresa: "To do small things with great love is much more important than doing many things in a hurried way."

∽

A quick review of the names the Missionaries of Charity choose for their centers of assistance reveals that these names are as simple as they are full of symbolism.

On more than one occasion, Mother Teresa said that she didn't spend much time looking for a name for her congregation. As the works of the congregation took shape, she thought Missionaries of Charity, being simple, would best define the people doing the work.

This fact is so much more appreciable if we consider that, with few exceptions, the titles of other religious institutions have become more and more elaborate with the passing of decades and centuries. The work founded by Mother Teresa, however—so recent that it will be only a half century old when this second millennium ends—gave evidence of a certain "disregard" for the need to be especially original. Mother Teresa was more concerned with identifying the works to be done. To some extent these works are not at all novel, insofar as they have strong roots in the gospel message of Jesus.

The name chosen for each project is usually the emblem of its aims. These aims are carried out in all of the initiatives that bear the signature of Mother Teresa: making concrete, in a genuine and simple way, genuine and simple Christianity.

It is interesting to note that all titles given to the foundations of the Missionaries of Charity are from the liturgy or from popular piety, such as "Morning Star," "Gift of Peace,"

"Home of Peace," "Queen of Peace Home," "House of Joy," "Immaculate Heart of Mary Home," and "Gift of Mary Home."

⌒

A person can't help noticing the sense of serene joy that is usu-ally reflected on the faces of the Missionaries of Charity. To smile and be happy when living in poverty-stricken surround-ings, with the attending suffering and human misery, presup-poses inner conditions that have more to do with a lively and steady faith than with any presumed lack of awareness. British journalist Malcolm Muggeridge noted in his book, *Something Beautiful for God*:

> What the poor need, Mother Teresa is fond of say-ing, even more than food and clothing and shelter (though they need these, too, desperately), is to be wanted. It is the outcast state their poverty imposes upon them that is the most agonizing. She has a place in her heart for them all. To her, they are all children of God for whom Christ died and so de-serving of all love. If God counts the hairs of each of their heads, if none are excluded from the salva-tion the crucifixion offers, who will venture to ex-clude them from earthly blessings and esteem; pro-nounce this life unnecessary, that one better termi-nated or never begun? I never experienced so per-fect a sense of human equality as with Mother Teresa among her poor. Her love for them, reflecting God's love, makes them equal, as brothers and sisters within a family are equal, however widely they dif-

fer in intellectual and other attainments, in physical beauty and grace.

Sentiment leads to philanthropy, which is all to the good. But a sense of philanthropy wasn't what Mother Teresa wanted to impart to her sisters and Co-Workers. Hers was an attitude of sustained service on behalf of the poor, whom she considered to be Christ himself; that's why Mother Teresa believed the poor deserved to be loved, not out of compassion per se but out of respect for the most profound part of his or her own being.

Nevertheless, the serene joy that can be seen in the faces of the Missionaries of Charity does not mean they don't wage inner battles and cry inside from time to time.

⌐

Each sister has a history. There is no reason to believe that any of the four thousand Missionaries of Charity have known constant happiness since they first felt the call to serve Jesus in the poor. On the contrary.

For example, it isn't unusual to hear of faithful and optimistic parents who joyfully accept the news that their daughter wants to join Mother Teresa. Nor is it unusual to hear of parents who do not understand or accept their daughter's call to join the Missionaries of Charity, even when their daughter is already professed. In fact, some parents—and even siblings—exhibit a distinct bias: "If we were talking about any other nuns, maybe; but with these? They don't even use automatic washers, and they live off alms. Who can assure me that some day my daughter won't be lacking the simple necessities?"

Opposition on the part of their families, and especially their parents, is a heavy cross for some Missionaries of Charity. There are many such stories, and one in particular best illustrates their commonality. A young woman who chose to become a Missionary of Charity contrary to her parents' cherished dreams for her. "How can you do this to us, now that your father and I are old?" her mother asked. "Do whatever you like but not this. If you insist on becoming a nun, be another kind of nun. We admire Mother Teresa, as you already know. But her group is for girls from India. For God's sake, no!"

Precisely; for God's sake. The young woman prayed that all, her mother especially, would come to understand and accept her decision. But on the day of her profession, the young novice's prayer had not been answered; her mother went "grumbling" to her daughter's "celebration."

Many who consecrate themselves to God believe that they will be granted whatever they pray for on the day of their profession. This young lady asked two things of Jesus: that she be worthy to save all the souls with whom she would come into contact with as a Missionary of Charity and that he would inspire her with adequate words to calm and reassure her mother. Following the ceremony, the words came: "Mama, aren't you happy to have Jesus as a son-in-law?"

Although there is no indication today that the young woman's mother has changed her attitude, this anonymous Missionary of Charity continues to have a very strong faith in God and does indeed touch the souls of those she serves.

～

In some cases, the obstacles encountered by certain candidates for the Missionaries of Charity come from within. One such case involved a thirty-year-old woman.

Despite the fact that Mother Teresa was the first Missionary of Charity whom the woman had known personally, she approached the novitiate full of doubts about whether "this" was truly for her. In her soul, a drama had been unchained:

> My desires were as strong as my repugnance and fear. In the middle, as an apparently mute witness, was Jesus. There were moments when I felt Jesus confront me. Then there were other times when I felt tempted to leave it all. These moments were followed by others when I recovered my calm within myself and with Jesus. But the day arrived, which I recall very well—although not the external reasons, if there were any—when I settled the matter. On that day, without having foreseen it, I felt suddenly infused with a profound calm which never again left me.

↜

There was a seminarian with a fine and gentle spirit who gave a helping hand in a soup kitchen run by the Missionaries of Charity. One cold evening, he offered lodging in his own home to a young immigrant from North Africa.

The following morning, the seminarian's guest didn't wait to eat the breakfast prepared for him. Instead, he hurriedly left—taking with him the seminarian's personal computer and other valuables. The incident became public knowledge, not because the seminarian spread the news but because he simply mentioned the burglary to one person who, in turn, told it to another, and so forth.

Naturally, those who knew about the incident were surprised when they spotted the young North African some evenings later in the soup kitchen where the seminarian kindly filled his plate. When asked about the situation, the seminarian replied, "Forget it. We've taken care of it," meaning that the repentant immigrant had admitted to selling the computer and the valuables and had sent the money to his needy mother.

The seminarian gave the man an additional small sum of money and again offered him lodging for the night. The young immigrant accepted the offer—and again, stole from his host.

Once news of the second incident got to be known, most people focused on the gall and ingratitude of the immigrant. Others, however, pondered the seminarian's good heart and trusting nature and saw there the true spirit of love.

∽

A person close to the spirit of Mother Teresa, a Co-Worker for years, says that the individual lives of the poor so often could be the makings of a plot for a good book.

For example, many of those who come to the soup kitchens or reside in the shelters of the Missionaries of Charity have been in jail. Some have passed through immense human degradation and have become depreciated and undone in body and spirit. Their histories vary, of course; many have suffered severely at the hands of others; others have suffered as a result of their own poor choices. Some have paid dearly with jail sentences, social ostracism, and alienation from their families.

But there is dignity in the present when the past is not questioned and judgment is not rendered. The present is possible for those who have committed crimes out of a lack of love and yet feel themselves redeemed from their crimes because of love offered.

How redeemed Edward must have felt. He had been a pickpocket, had evidently spent time in jail, and had come to the Missionaries of Charity for help in his dying days.

Edward seldom spoke of his history. Rather, he received the gift of the present within the loving environment offered by the sisters. He used his limited energy to make objects of art that he sold or selflessly gave away.

Edward died a tranquil death on Christmas Eve. Although the sisters had little information about Edward, they did know that he had a married brother. They decided to send a note to the brother to notify him of Edward's death.

When the message bearer delivered the news to Edward's brother, the response was cruel but perhaps understandable: "For us, that person died a long time ago."

Edward was buried on December 26. His burial was simple, and few people were present. Among them were four Missionaries of Charity and several of Edward's roommates from the Home for the Dying. All were convinced that a brother had returned to the home of his Father.

HER FRIEND MALCOLM

Although she was a humble woman who had no desire to be observed or esteemed, Mother Teresa had millions of admirers from all nationalities, professions, and religious creeds. How often have we heard the question, "Who is the person you most admire in all the world?" and the response, "Mother Teresa of Calcutta"?

The humanistic-Christian cause that Mother Teresa incarnated more than anyone else during the twentieth century has been captured and preserved for centuries to come by her many admirers. Among them are certain individuals who have been able to communicate not only what Mother Teresa did but who she was. There isn't enough space here to mention all of them. No historical account of Mother Teresa is complete, however, without due credit and appreciation being given to the British journalist Malcolm Muggeridge, Mother Teresa's first biographer.

Former spy, veteran of combat, war correspondent, and special envoy to a variety of countries caught in conflict and war, Muggeridge was endowed with a pen that won its good name and respect in the war trenches of journalism. Throughout his long career, his writings were published by the greatest presses of the United Kingdom. He honored *The Guardian, The Daily Telegraph, The Evening News,* and *The Times* with chronicles and articles. His credibility and his capacity for the "dramatic" created a demand for him as a commentator on both radio and television programs of the British Broadcasting Company.

Muggeridge possessed a skepticism common to intellectuals who are experienced in the ways of the world. Although officially he was an adherent of the Anglican Church, Muggeridge was neither a believer nor an atheist. Rather, he considered himself something more rational: an agnostic open to admiring authentic witness. Muggeridge had occasion to admire "authentic witness" when he found himself on assignment in Calcutta, India, during the early sixties.

At that time, Mother Teresa was hardly known in the West,

even in the Catholic media. On his return to England, Muggeridge convinced his bosses at the BBC that there was newsworthy material in the life and work of this little-known Catholic religious. His original radio interview with Mother Teresa in 1960 had involved nothing more than catching her during a stop in London on a return trip to India from the United States. Now, Muggeridge wanted to do something more in depth about Mother Teresa and her work among the poor in her own environment.

Muggeridge's proposed television documentary (the first ever to be produced about Mother Teresa) required great logistic development. Above all, Muggeridge had to find a way to help Mother Teresa overcome her reluctance to cameras focusing on her work. Consequently, he asked the archbishop of Westminster, Cardinal Carmel Heenan, for a letter of recommendation. The archbishop obliged. His letter said just the right things and pointed out that Muggeridge's documentary "could do much good for souls."

Once Mother Teresa's resistance was overcome by Cardinal Heenan's comments, she forgot about the cameras and went to work with her usual naturalness—a naturalness that gave the documentary a sense of total veracity.

Although riddled with the usual technical difficulties, the filming required no second and third "takes." The authenticity of the subject matter seemed to offset any production shortcomings. In fact, Muggeridge came to suspect that a miracle had occurred. He could not otherwise explain how well many of the scenes reproduced.

Because of its technical inadequacies, however, and the "rationalistic prejudice" then prevalent against this kind of topic, the documentary was scheduled as filler on an uneventful autumn Sunday afternoon in the British Isles. For once, the demanding television audience paid more attention to content than to technical quality, and the unforeseen occurred. The public demanded that the program be broadcast again at a more reasonable and "prime time" hour.

Although the documentary made no pitch for money, Muggeridge and the BBC received numerous checks totaling twenty thousand pounds. The donations were earmarked for "the nun in the white-and-blue sari" and her work.

Using material from the radio interview and the television documentary, Muggeridge published a book about Mother Teresa and her work. The book was extremely successful in English and in the twenty-some languages into which it was immediately translated.

Malcolm Muggeridge's contribution to Mother Teresa and her work was as fundamental as it was decisive. Fundamental because it was a pioneering effort; it placed Mother Teresa's work at the starting point for its extension outside of India. Decisive because Muggeridge's ability to communicate—the consistency of his writing and television work—gave Mother Teresa's work widespread credibility.

At the time of the interviews, Muggeridge wasn't Catholic and didn't feel the slightest inclination to convert. In *Something Beautiful for God*, Muggeridge asserts:

> I never met anyone more memorable. Just meeting
> her for a fleeting moment makes an ineffaceable
> impression. I have known people burst into tears
> when she goes, though it was only from a tea party
> where their acquaintance with her amounted to no
> more than receiving her smile.

It is interesting to learn Muggeridge's point of view regarding the role of religion in Mother Teresa's life. In his book, he reflects on the subject:

> For Mother Teresa, faith is a personal relationship with God and the incarnate Christ; the Mass the spiritual food which sustains her, without which, as she told me, she could not get through one single day or hour of the life of dedication she has chosen; the Church something she belongs to, serves, and obeys as revealing and fulfilling God's purposes on earth. The various controversies and conflicts now shaking the Church scarcely touch her; they will pass, she says, and the Church will remain to perform its divinely inspired and directed function.
>
> I know that Mother Teresa cannot understand the hesitations and doubts which make it impossible for me to accept her way of looking at the Church's present predicament, or to see it as other than an institution which a mortal hierarchy and priesthood can make or mar, sustain or let collapse.

Mother Teresa always desired that her friend Malcolm might come into the Catholic faith. The British journalist, for his part, was conscious of such a desire, but he resisted conversion for a long time.

> There are few things I should rather do than please her. So much, that it almost amounts to a temptation to accept her guidance in the matter of entering the Church just because it is hers. Yet everything

tells me that this would be wrong...for me, it would
be fraudulent, and we cannot, dear Mother Teresa,
buy faith—least of all faith—with counterfeit urges.
I know perfectly well that, however much I long for
it to be otherwise, the bell does not ring for me.
Nor is there a place for me at the altar rail where
they kneel to receive the Body of Christ. I should be
an outsider there, too. The Church, after all, is an
institution with a history; a past and a future. It went
on crusades, it set up an inquisition, it installed scan-
dalous popes, and countenanced monstrous iniq-
uities. Institutionally speaking, these are perfectly
comprehensible, and even, in earthly terms, excus-
able. In the mouthpiece of God on earth, belonging, not just to history, but to everlasting truth, they
are not to be defended. At least, not by me.

In those days—the end of the sixties—Muggeridge obviously
had serious personal reasons for not following the Catholic
faith. Nevertheless, Mother Teresa continued to pray that those
reasons might disappear, and it seems inevitable that this conversion would come to pass.

On November 27, 1982, Malcolm Muggeridge and his wife,
Kitty Dobbs, took the definitive step and became Catholic at a
Mass presided over by the bishop of Brighton, Monsignor
Cormac Murphy-O'Connor. Mother Teresa couldn't be at the
ceremony, but her spirit was felt in the presence of Malcolm's
special guests: a group of children with handicaps. The journalist was seventy-nine years old and had retired to East Sussex, in the south of England.

Man of communication that he was, Muggeridge agreed to

write a book about the change effected in his life. Titled *Conversion: A Spiritual Journey*, the book was published in February 1988 by Collins. In it, Muggeridge admits that his entrance into the Church did not procure for him "so much jubilation as a profound peace; a sense of returning home, of tying up the threads of a lost life; of responding to a bell that had been sounding for a long time; of occupying a seat long vacant at the table."

Muggeridge's book on his "spiritual journey to conversion" was reviewed in an English daily by Bishop Murphy-O'Connor. After reading the book, the bishop noted that Muggeridge's conversion "had been a series of events, the gradual unfolding of a rich interior life, of ups and downs, of alternate states of exaltation and despair."

The man who had written so much was, at the end, blind. Muggeridge himself said, "Like Macbeth, I have lived too long; I want to say, sufficiently. Writing is something like a blind walk; a sort of deep uncertainty. You can lighten those limitations that wound you, or you can laugh about them. I am blind now, but Kitty reads for me, patiently, for hours and hours."

When asked what advice he had for someone who might come to him in search of light, Muggeridge responded, "Something which Bishop Fulton Sheen told me when I visited him in his apartment in New York two days before his death. He told me: 'Christianity is overwhelmed, but not Christ.' I always found his message very thought-provoking."

Malcolm Muggeridge, British journalist, social critic, convert to Catholicism, and Mother Teresa's first biographer, died November 14, 1992, at the age of eighty-seven.

Chapter 8

CALLED A SAINT
WHILE STILL AMONG US

The least we can say about Mother Teresa—keeping in mind her day of birth (August 27, 1910)—is that she has lived longer than the average person from her generation. Actually, her longevity has been nothing short of miraculous.

The circumstances under which she grew up didn't favor her reaching such an advanced age. In her teenage years, Mother Teresa's health was rather fragile, so her mother always made sure that young Teresa took it easy in the summertime. As a result, Mother Teresa spent a great deal of time relaxing on a hill close to the Shrine of Our Lady of Letnice, to whom she felt very devoted.

When her health failed again during the mid forties, she spent an entire year recovering. But we cannot rule out the possibility that her decision to leave behind her happy life as a loyal Missionary Sister of Our Lady of Loreto aggravated her condition. At the risk of financial uncertainty, she embraced a life solely dependent on her faith in divine Providence, following the path that, in her own words, "clearly showed me where I had to go, but not how to get there."

From that time on, she has enjoyed relatively good health— even during the extremely busy early years of her congregation. She has even said, "God has blessed me with good health. It was a sign that he wanted me to be of service to him."

But the passing of the years has brought some bad times. After turning seventy, she began to suffer from continuing heart problems. In 1980, while staying in Rome, she had to be hospitalized for two and a half months. Although the nursing staff went out of their way to make her stay as pleasant as possible, she apparently didn't like to see herself as the center of attention. What she wished was to serve the poor, not to be served. She felt uncomfortable and was eager to leave the clinic. In jest, the Italian clinic's staff labeled her a "difficult patient."

In 1983 her health failed her again. This time she was hospitalized with chronic angina pectoris.

In September 1989 the sisters closest to Mother Teresa had her admitted to Woodlands Nursing Home in Calcutta. The medical staff noted that her health had worsened due to her busy travel and work schedules. To correct the arhythmia she suffered due to a blocked artery, she was fitted with a pacemaker. To be discharged, she was told, she would have to cut down on her travels, eventually refraining from them completely. Mother Teresa followed the doctors and sisters' advice only so long as her workload allowed. In December, barely three months later, she had to return to Woodlands Nursing Home.

In December 1991, after spending Christmas with her sisters and the poor of Tijuana, Mexico, Mother Teresa contracted pneumonia. She was transported to a hospital in La Jolla, California, where the medical staff performed an angioplasty to open her coronary arteries. At the same time she was diagnosed with anemia and malnutrition.

In May 1993, Mother Teresa fell down while walking to the chapel in the house of Saint Gregory al Celio, during a stay in Rome. She suffered three broken ribs—and was hospitalized in the same clinic where she had been labeled a "difficult patient."

Because of her heart problems, Mother Teresa has been hospitalized in New Delhi and Calcutta on other occasions. In some instances, malaria fever complicated her condition. And once a street dog sank its teeth into her arm when she knelt down to feed it. As a precaution, she had to get a rabies shot.

At the end of 1996, due to her failing health, Mother Teresa resigned as superior general of the Missionaries of Charity.

HER ARMY OF FOLLOWERS

The Congregation of the Missionaries of Charity Sisters began in 1950, in India. Fifteen years had to pass before congregation houses could open in other countries. That's how long it took for the Vatican to grant Mother Teresa's congregation permission to serve the rest of the world.

Without any publicity efforts—their only advertising the genuine joy in their faces from serving Jesus in the poor—the sisters soon attracted young candidates from England, France, Italy, Spain, Germany, Switzerland, Holland, Canada, the United States, and other countries. Many of them had been college students or had been well-paid and highly skilled professionals: doctors, nurses, flight attendants, teachers, bank employees, publicists…

The number of women who wish to follow Mother Teresa has continued to grow, especially after she was awarded the Nobel Prize for Peace in 1979—the only Catholic nun so honored. Today few countries do not have a Missionaries of Charity house. In many countries, including the United States, Italy, Spain, England, Germany, France, Portugal, Mexico, Venezuela, Argentina, and Colombia, the congregation boasts more than one house.

In most instances, Mother Teresa has opened new houses at the request of the local Catholic hierarchy. Still, the requests have been so many that she has been able to fulfill only a small percentage of them. In other cases, requests to open houses and shelters for the poor have come from government leaders themselves when religious organizations were lacking or disapproved by the government. Such has been the case in Cuba, Nicaragua under the Sandinistas, the former Soviet Union, Rumania, Hungary, South Yemen, and other countries.

In 1980 Mother Teresa, in the company of four sisters, personally opened a house in her hometown of Skopje, Macedonia. The occasion prompted her to share the following quip with her former fellow citizens: "Macedonia gave the Missionaries of Charity one sister; the congregation returns the favor with four." In Albania, the Missionaries of Charity have seven houses, staffed by many local sisters.

THE TWENTIETH CENTURY'S MOST CELEBRATED WOMAN

Some people manage to achieve a dubious kind of fame after having worked ceaselessly for it, or after receiving help from others interested only in promoting their own interests. Mother

Teresa has never done anything just to become famous; rather, she has worked continuously to do what has needed to be done. Despite her mostly low-key manner, her work has made her so well known that she has become for the world a paradigm of philanthropy, the epitome of Christian charity.

Mother's Teresa's intense work on behalf of others has also brought her a life of unpredictability. Without a doubt, she has never wasted a minute of it, and she has never had a minute to waste as she has confronted the worst cases of human tragedy resulting from accidents and disasters of both natural and human origin.

Without recourse to the material resources that the rest of us consider necessities, and always unconcerned for her own well-being, Mother Teresa has always found her support in Jesus. Her wholehearted love for the Lord enables her to see him present among those who suffer the most, and he has always provided what she has needed to carry out his work.

In working only for the love of Jesus, Mother Teresa has spurned fame and fortune. Although she continues to live a life of poverty, she is unaccountably rich in the love of the Lord. And she is perhaps the most famous woman of the century. That's the paradox that will always follow one of the most admired women in history.

A long time may pass before another Mother Teresa appears in this world. After all, her life has been—dare one say it?—a miracle: the miracle of the gospel message in action. That is why millions who do not even share her faith call her "saint."

When she is no longer among us, the Church may take many years to make the people's verdict official—but that won't matter. In the eyes of those whose lives she has touched with love, she is already a genuine saint.

NOTES

Chapter 1: Out of India

1. Mother Dengel held Mother Teresa and her work in great esteem. As long as the Medical Mission Sisters retained the hospital, they were always ready to help Mother Teresa and her congregation. Years later, Mother Dengel and her congregation abandoned Patna and donated the building and the grounds to Mother Teresa.

2. The International Association of Co-Workers of Mother Teresa is open to members of any religious creed.

Chapter 2: A "Pencil" in the Hands of God

1. Eileen Egan, *Such a Vision of the Street: Mother Teresa—The Spirit and the Work*, Sidgwick and Jackson, London, 1985, p. 136.

2. Among the numerous titles given to John XXIII, "Pope of the Council" is most familiar. Protestant pastor Marc Boegner notes, however, that John Baptist Montini (Pope Paul VI), who perhaps would not have had the courage to convoke the council, was pope when the council came to an end. Over the years, the human and intellectual greatness of Paul VI and his influence on the history of the Church and humanity have been increasingly acknowledged. His cause for beatification was introduced in May 1993.

3. The author finds this episode similar to one he witnessed. As a gift, Mother Teresa had received a parcel of land in a major Euporean capital. She planned to build a home for the dying on the land but could not secure permission of the municipal government. She visited the mayor, who promised her to "do all that was possible" within municipal ordinances. The mayor kept his word, and a few days later the sisters were granted a construction permit. When Mother Teresa received news of the permission, she was at an airport. She quickly wrote a note of thanks on a piece of notebook paper and signed off with her customary "God bless you." The mayor, a socialist and agnostic, framed the simple note and hung it in his office at city hall, where it remained until the end of his term.

4. Such a condition is formulated in Article 102 of the Constitution of the Missionaries of Charity: "Before making the foundation, the Superior General or her delegate must visit the place to ascertain conditions of living and work."

5. The Joseph Kennedy, Jr., Foundation Award included $15,000. With this money, Mother Teresa launched a center for special children in the area of Dum Dum, near the airport of Calcutta. She decided to link the name of the donors with that of the center: Nirmala Kennedy Center.

6. On October 6, 1988, the formal process for the beatification and canonization of Cardinal Terence J. Cooke was introduced by his successor in the New York See, John J. O'Connor.

Chapter 3: Called to Serve the King of the Universe

1. The name "Agnes" is related to the Greek word *agne,* which means "chaste," and the Latin word *agnus,* which means "lamb." According to tradition, the son of the prefect of Rome fell in love with thirteen-year-old Agnes and proposed marriage. She refused. The crestfallen young man stirred up the anger in his father who, when he discovered the woman to be a Christian, had her beheaded. Her feast is celebrated on January 21. In iconography she appears with a lamb at her feet.

2. Most biographies of Mother Teresa of Calcutta note her sister, Aga, to be the older of the two girls. Unless Aga's headstone is

wrong, however, she was the youngest of the three surviving children born to Nikolle Bojaxhiu and Drana Bernai-Bojaxhiu.

3. Drana Bernai: 1889–1972; Aga: 1913-1973. These dates are inscribed on the headstones marking the women's simple graves in the cemetery in the Albanian capital.

4. Nikolle Bojaxhiu's mother owned a weaving workshop. His young widow may have been inspired by this family precedent.

5. The following conversation is the author's reconstruction.

6. At profession, Betika Kanjc chose the name Mary Magdalene. She remained in the community of the Sisters of Our Lady of Loreto the rest of her life.

7. In spite of this, the beatification of Mary Ward has been put on hold.

8. Mother Teresa frequently expressed appreciation to the Sisters of Loreto, who supported and nurtured her vocation during her years as a member of their community. She eloquently states her sentiments in the prologue to *Mary Ward through Her Writings:* "Mary Ward constitutes a gift of God to the Church. She uncovered, especially for women, a new dimension. She made it possible that women could participate in the field of education, and that likewise they could prepare themselves to assume a new task within the Church….Profoundly grateful to Loreto for the twenty years spent working and praying among the Sisters, I ask that each one of them grow in sanctity, following very closely Mary Ward, especially in her love as much for the Virgin as for those whom she served."

Chapter 4: Heart and Hands to the Task

1. Subashini Das chose the foundress' baptismal name, Agnes, when she professed her vows as a Missionary of Charity. She enjoyed a great confidence with Mother Teresa and became the first director of Nirmal Hriday. With Sister Gertrude, the second woman to join the order, she accompanied Mother Teresa to Oslo to accept the Nobel Prize for Peace in 1979.

2. The Archdiocese of Calcutta advanced the money as a loan to the Missionaries of Charity. In small increments, Mother Teresa gradually paid off the loan.

3. About the formation program for the Missionaries of Charity,

Cardinal John O'Connor writes: "In no way does a young woman simply enter and become a Missionary of Charity without further ado. The relgious and doctrinal formation in the essentials of the religious life is profound and prolonged. The laborious work, more than simply difficult, is demanding. Before a woman is considered for the vows, she must learn to embrace those who are covered with sores and worms, and to teach them to love Jesus with sincere joy. I also heard the criticism that some young women enter because the passage represents for them a step up from an even worse poverty. I have also heard that only the ignorant and those who have never had the opportunity for studies ask to enter into the Missionaries of Charity. There is nothing so stupid. A minimal contact is enough to convince one that among them there are those who have entered with careers completed, with university studies, who have set aside highly valued professions in the fields of communication, medicine, even entertainment, who are completely integrated Missionaries of Charity and who carry out the same work as Mother Teresa. But even when such a situation does not occur, if culture and high-tech specialization were conditions for apostolic work, one would have to conclude that no one told Jesus at the time he chose his twelve apostles" ("The Most Powerful Woman," *Catholic New York,* October 31, 1985).

4. Adoption is an aspect of the work of the Missionaries of Charity. The complexity that surrounds adoptions is primarily due to the legal limitations imposed by certain countries on such operations. Nonetheless, Mother Teresa and the Missionaries of Charity have been responsible for hundreds of successful adoptions. It wasn't unusual for Mother Teresa to meet one of these adopted children—an adult and married—in a joyful reunion. In all their adoption negotiations, the Missionaries of Charity act with scrupulous regard for the law, while keeping the rights of the children as their greatest value.

5. The opening of centers in other Indian cities and eventually in other countries was conditioned by juridic-canonical circumstances. The congregation was initially authorized as a diocesan "experiment," limited to the jurisdiction of the archbishop of Calcutta (*Decree of Erection* of October 7, 1950). As a result of

request from other Indian bishops, the congregation was permitted to establish daughter houses in other dioceses of the confederation. With the *Decree of Praise* of February 1, 1965, which sanctioned its validity for the entire Catholic world, the congregation could establish houses in any diocese in the world. The first bishop to make such a request was Monsignor Benítez of the Diocese of Barquisimeto, Venezuela. Each new house established by the Missionaries of Charity has quickly filled with novices, which prompted Mother Teresa to believe so strongly in Providence: "If God keeps sending us vocations, it is a sign that he wants us to use them for his glory. For that reason, we maintain the rhythm of opening new houses without stopping." During the first several years after Mother Teresa was awarded the Nobel Prize for Peace, the congregation opened an average of twenty-five new houses a year.

6. Mother Teresa founded the Missionaries of Charity with the intention of forfeiting ownership of material goods. Thus, when she acquired the first house, she wanted to claim it simply in the name of the Church. Her juridic-canonical advisor, Father Celeste Van Exem, intervened and explained that because the Holy See was not recognized as a state by India, it was impossible to give legal formalization to her desire.

7. Jacqueline de Decker must be given special credit for the role she played as a Co-Worker. Mother Teresa met Jacqueline at the hospital at Patna. Although Jacqueline felt herself called to serve the poor in India, as was Mother Teresa, her poor health kept her from realizing her dream. Instead, she supported Mother Teresa's work from afar as a spiritual link and was significantly influential is bringing others to do the same.

Chapter 5: A Platform for Life

1. It is appropriate to recall an anecdote narrated by Mother Teresa's friend and benefactor, Jesuit Celeste Van Exem: "At times, Mother Teresa seemed exhausted by the great number of invitations which she received on behalf of men of the Church. She got to the point of complaining about it with the pope: 'Holy Father, there are so many cardinals and bishops who invite me to come to meetings to speak. I can't; it's too much. I owe my time first of

all to my Sisters, scattered now all over the world. I'm old. I'm sick. Give me authorization so that when some cardinal or bishop invites me I can say to him that the Holy Father has prohibited me.' It seems John Paul II promised her, smiling, that he would think about it." Father Van Exem continued with a certain irony, "I believe he is still thinking about it." (Quoted in Navin Chawla, *Mother Teresa*, Sinclair Stevenson, London, 1993, p. 188.)

Following are the addresses of
Missionaries of Charity houses in the
United States and Canada:

818 N. Collington Ave.
Baltimore, MD 21205
Tel. (410) 732-6056

3310 Wheeler Rd., S.E.
Washington, DC 20032
Tel. (202) 562-6890

401 Quincy St.
Boston, MA 02125
Tel. (617) 288-4182

2800 Otis St., N.E.
Wahington, DC 20018
Tel. (202) 269-3313

4835 Lincoln St.
Detroit, MI 48208
Tel. (313) 831-1028

1014 South Oak St.
Little Rock, AR 72204
Tel. (501) 663-3596

168 Sussex Ave.
Newark, NJ 07103
Tel. (201) 483-0165

727 N.W. 17th St.
Miami, FL 33136
Tel. (305) 545-5699

335 E. 145th St.
Bronx, NY 10451
Tel. (212) 292-0019

2234 W. Washington Blvd.
Chicago, IL 60612
Tel. (312) 421-0038

406 West 127th St.
Harlem, NY 10027
Tel. (718) 222-7229

PO Box 883 (400 Cove Street)
Jenkins, KY 41537
Tel. (606) 832-4284

657 Washington St.
Manhattan, NY 10014
Tel. (212) 645-0587

715 East Blvd.
Baton Rouge, LA 70802
Tel. (504) 343-2138

630 De Kalb St.
Norristown, PA 19401
Tel. (610) 277-5962

911 St. John St.
Lafayette, LA 70501
Tel. (318) 233-3929

3629 Cottage
St. Louis, MO 63113
Tel. (314) 533-2777

700 N. 7th St.
Memphis, TN 38107
Tel. (901) 527-4947

2704 Harlandale Ave.
Dallas, TX 75216
Tel. (214) 374-3351

1414 S. 17th Ave.
Phoenix, AZ 85007
Tel. (602) 258-5504

312 29th St.
San Francisco, CA 94131
Tel. (415) 647-1889

974 Valencia St.
San Francisco, CA 94110
Tel. (415) 821-9687

1596 Fulton St.
San Francisco, CA 94117
Tel. (415) 563-9446

207 E. Wilson Ave.
Gallup, NM 87301
Tel. (505) 722-5261

St. Patrick's Mission
PO Box 267
Vanderwagen, NM 87326
Tel. (505) 778-5740

1840 Grant St.
Denver, CO 80203
Tel. (303) 860-8040

10950 California Ave.
Lynwood, CA 90262
Tel. (213) 635-3264

506 Hancock St.
Peoria, IL 61603
Tel. (309) 674-7160

Gift of Mary
2714 W. 9th St.
Chester, PA 19013
Tel. (610) 494-4724

CANADA

356 Pritchard Ave.
Winnipeg, Manitoba R2W 2J6
Tel. (204) 582-2773

185 Dunn Ave.
Toronto, Ontario N6K 2S1
Tel. (416) 537-1391

2465 Rue Champagne
Montreal, Quebec H2K 2G9
Tel. (514) 524-6372

4737 44th Ave.
PO Box 2077
St. Paul, Alberta TDA 3AO
Tel. (403) 645-2968

2475 E. 48th Ave.
Vancouver, B.C. V5S 1G5
Tel. (604) 322-6840

INDEX

ABOUT THE AUTHOR

José Luis González-Balado is a Spanish journalist and author of books on Pope John XXIII, Pope John Paul II, and Dom Helder Cámara, as well as several others on Mother Teresa. He served as Spanish coordinator of the Co-Workers and was among those who helped the Missionaries of Charity establish a home for the poor in Spain. He has known Mother Teresa since 1969.